Lavender

HUNDREDS OF EVERYDAY USES

Publisher's Note:
All reasonable care has been exercised by the author and publisher to ensure that the tips and remedies included in this guide are simple and safe. However, it is important to note that all uses of lavender should be practised with caution and a doctor's, or relevant professional's, advice should be sought if in any doubt or before any topical or medicinal usage – the advice in this book is not a replacement for that of a doctor. The author, editors and publisher take no responsibility for any consequences of any application which results from reading the information contained herein.

A note on measurements:
Please note also that the measurements provided in this book are presented as metric/imperial/US–cups practical equivalents.

This is a **FLAME TREE** book
First published in 2012

Publisher and Creative Director: Nick Wells
Project Editor: Laura Bulbeck
Picture Research: Lydia Good and Laura Bulbeck
Art Director: Mike Spender
Layout Design: Jane Ashley
Digital Design and Production: Chris Herbert

Special thanks to Gina Steer for writing the recipe text.

12 14 16 15 13

1 3 5 7 9 10 8 6 4 2

FLAME TREE PUBLISHING
Crabtree Hall, Crabtree Lane
Fulham, London SW6 6TY
United Kingdom

www.flametreepublishing.com

© 2012 Flame Tree Publishing Ltd

ISBN 978-0-85775-617-6

A CIP Record for this book is available from the British Library upon request.

Every effort has been made to contact copyright holders. We apologise in advance for any omissions and would be pleased to insert the appropriate acknowledgement in subsequent editions of this publication.

Printed in China

The following images are courtesy of Shutterstock and © the following contributors: 1 & 112 & 128r, 140b, 38 & 60 & 118 & 149 & 168 marilyn barbone; 3 & 10 & 17 & 20 & 48 & 114 & 138 & 172, 90 Elena Schweitzer; 5 & 54 Svetlana Lukienko; 6 Tamara Kulikova; 7 Johan_R; 8 Dmitriy Shironosov; 9 Bethan Collins; 11 Andreas G. Karelias; 12 & 82t & 124 & 162, 147l & 150 Diana Taliun; 13 BeaB; 14 angelakatharina; 15t Olga K; 15b, 18 Maren Wulf; 16 Giancarlo Liguori; 19 Peter Radacsi; 21, 137B Ingrid Balabanova; 22 Ivan Ponomarev; 23 Zaneta Baranowska ; 24t LiliGraphie; 24b Sergej Razvodovskij; 25t viki2win; 25b, 115 beboy; 26 winnond; 27 Patrick Wang; 28 & 55t Fotonium; 29 Dmitry Naumov; 31 Henry Steven; 32b PeterG; 32t Sinisa Botas; 33t djem; 33b Serena Carminati; 34, 157, 158 Andreja Donko; 35 terekhov igor; 36 Sandra Cunningham; 37r photosync; 37l RPM.Photo; 39 oliveromg; 40 michaeljung; 41t, 85t kotomiti; 41b Joe Gough; 42 2happy; 43t Andre Klopper; 43b shutswis; 44r Daniel Krylov; 44l Julia Zakharova; 45, 75L, 79b, 84 wavebreakmedia ltd; 46b Murat Subatli; 46t Serg64; 47b nito; 47t Tifonimages; 49 Julija Sapic; 50 auremar; 51t, 68t, 68b, 161, 185 matka_Wariatka; 51b Skyline; 52 Yuganov Konstantin; 53t Danijel Micka; 53b Vatikaki; 55b Simon Bratt; 56t gcpics; 56b Nikolai Tsvetkov; 57 andersphoto; 58 & 82b Serg Salivon; 59 oksix; 61 & 166 Danny Smythe; 62, 77, 100, 110 Valua Vitaly; 63 & 74 & 152 & 30 Neirfy; 64 discpicture; 65, 69, 89, 167 joanna wnuk; 66t Fedulova Olga; 66b svehlik; 67 Katia Vasileva; 70 foto.fritz; 71 Kamira; 72 altafulla; 73, 93 Piotr Marcinski; 75r Yaro; 76, 113 Elena Elisseeva; 78 AISPIX by Image Source; 79t S_L; 80 samotrebizan; 81 Stephanie Swartz; 83b Cgissemann; 83t Dmitry Melnikov; 85b Monkey Business Images; 86t Dmitry Lobanov; 86b KULISH VIKTORIIA; 87 Layland Masuda; 88, 98, 97 Yuri Arcurs; 91 Michal Kowalski; 92t Bayanova Svetlana; 92b Catalin Petolea; 94 konzeptm; 95 Christo; 96 Phil Date; 99 tarog; 101 Ana Blazic Pavlovic; 102 Olga Miltsova; 103t Andresr; 103b kaarsten; 104 Melianiaka Kanstantsin; 105 DenisNata; 106 Ivaschenko Roman; 107 chantal de bruijne; 108t Anderson; 109, 160 mythja; 111 Amy Planz; 116t Lijuan Guo; 116b Shutterstock; 117 LI CHAOSHU; 119 cynoclub; 120 Dorottya Mathe; 121 Andrey Kekyalyaynen; 122 & 126t Danny Smythe; 123 Dasha Petrenko; 125 Christopher Elwell; 126b Alexander Raths; 126c Scott Latham; 127 Graeme Dawes ; 128l Nic Neish; 129 johnbraid; 130 Alison Hancock; 131b bogdan ionescu; 131t mayer kleinostheim; 132 Iuri; 133l Imageman; 133r Shebeko; 134 daizuoxin; 135 Gudrun Muenz; 136 fotohunter; 137t Julietphotography; 139 Boyan Dimitrov; 140t Markuso; 142 Mark Bridger; 145 Gina Smith; 146B DWPhoto; 146T Isabella Pfenninger; 147r Brent Hofacker; 148 freya-photographer; 151 Symbiot; 153 Aprilphoto; 154 Sunny Forest; 155, 164 Art_Maric; 156 Lukiyanova Natalia / frenta; 159 pgaborphotos; 163 Nolte Lourens; 165 Lambros Kazan; 169 Miguel Azevedo e Castro; 170 Cora Mueller; 171 jozette Tomassen; 173 Krzysztof Slusarczyk; 174 Iulia Vaculiosteanu; 179 Mshev; 181 Simone van den Berg; 183 Ksju; 187 Letterberry; and courtesy of Alamy and © the following: 175 Teubner Foodfoto/Bon Appetit; 177 Tim Hill; 189 Lutterbeck, Barbara/Bon Appetit; and courtesy of Wikimedia Commons (via the Creative Commons Attribution–Share Alike 3.0 Unported license) and the following supplier: 141 Viswaprabha

Lavender

HUNDREDS OF EVERYDAY USES

Jo Waters

**FLAME TREE
PUBLISHING**

Contents

Introduction

Lavender is probably one of the Western world's most popular flowering plants. It has been described as the quintessential herb, because of its all-round beauty, fragrance and downright usefulness. Widely grown for its heady aromatic scent, pretty purple flowers, valuable essential oil and a multitude of practical uses in natural medicine, beauty, household cleaning and craft, lavender really is one of nature's wonder plants.

Lavender Through the Ages

Lavender's uses have been documented since ancient Egyptian and Roman times, for everything from embalming bodies to perfuming Roman baths. Thousands of years later it is still being used for hundreds of everyday purposes.

What's in a Name?

The word lavender is believed by some to be derived from the Medieval Latin *lavare* (to wash). Another possible origin is the Latin word *livendula*, which means livid or bluish.

The World's Favourite Herb

There are over 35 different types of lavender, each producing beautiful flowers in summer. Lavender belongs to the same botanical family as mint, thyme, sage, basil and rosemary.

Grows Around the Globe

Lavender is a xerophyte, meaning that it is a plant adapted to thrive in dry conditions. It can grow in the Atlantic islands, North Africa, North America, the Mediterranean, India and Arabia, as well as Australia, Japan and New Zealand.

The Versatile Plant

Lavender truly is one of the most versatile plants on the planet and this is reflected in popular culture: the French painter Monet painted the famous purple fields of Provence; Marilyn Monroe said she slept in nothing but Yardley's English lavender; and the American novelist Alice Hoffman wrote in her novel *Practical Magic*, 'There's a few things I've learned in life: always throw salt over your left shoulder, keep rosemary by your garden gate, plant lavender for good luck, and fall in love whenever you can.'

Heaven's Scent

Lavender is one of the most widely used perfumes in the world, used to scent everything from soaps, shampoos and bubble bath to washing powders, furniture polish, household disinfectants and even moth balls. It's been described as having 'a green hay-like sweetness' which gives 'fruity aspects' to perfumes. For many, it's simply the smell of a summer's day.

For a Good Night's Sleep

The herb is associated with inducing relaxation and sleepiness. Dried flowers are sewn into muslin bags and either tied to the bedpost or placed under the head. Alternatively, bed linen can be laundered in lavender-scented fabric conditioners.

Handy For the Home

Lavender is a natural disinfectant and its scent masks the clinical smell of cleaning agents, so it's often added to furniture polishes. It's great for repelling moths, scenting drawers and killing mould (if mixed with white vinegar, *see* page 46). Its pleasant fragrance is also useful to incorporate in handicrafts.

Great For Beauty Products

Lavender's astringent properties make it a good component for facial toners, as it can help constrict the skin's pores. Lavender is also used in anti–dandruff shampoos, face creams and deodorizing products.

Lucky Lavender

Lavender also occupies a special place in folklore: it's said to have got its fragrance when Mary laid baby Jesus's clothes to dry on it. Other tales say it guards against evil spirits and ghosts, and acts as a lucky talisman. In the sixteenth and seventeenth centuries it was even used to protect against cholera and the plague.

All About Lavender

What Makes Up Lavender?

A recent chemical analysis published in 2010 has revealed that between 98 and 99 per cent of all lavender varieties contain the same 45 compounds. However, the two major constituents are linalool, which gives lavender oil its distinctive floral smell, and linalyl acetate, which occurs in many flowers and spices and has an anti-inflammatory effect.

Structure

Chemical Make-Up

Other constituents include **camphor** and **eucalyptol**, both used as decongestants to clear the nose and ease breathing. Linalool is a naturally occurring form of alcohol found in 200 different plant species. It has a pleasant floral odour and is also used as an ingredient in insect repellents. Research has confirmed lavender oils have antibacterial properties and a strong antioxidant effect.

Physical Make-Up

The lavender flower is made up of two parts:

Corolla: The petals or florets are most often purple through to lilac and some are white.

Calyx: This is a tube-like structure that joins the flower to the stem and is where dried lavender gets its colour.

Varieties

A Multitude of Choices

There are at least 30 types of lavender, each with their own distinctive flower, foliage and scent. There are lots of complicated classification systems and we don't have the space to list them all here, but here is a potted guide to some of the most popular.

Lavandula latifolia

Lavandula latifolia is a Mediterranean, grass-like lavender, also known as spike lavender or Portuguese lavender. It grows in Portugal, southern France, Spain, Italy and the Balkans. It has a more pungent, camphor smell than English lavender.

Lavandula × intermedia

These plants are hybrids of English lavender and *Lavandula latifolia*, combining the hardiness of the former with the heat tolerance of the latter. They need a sheltered sunny position to thrive but are prized for being disease-resistant and their high yield of deep violet flowers and strong scent.

Lavandula

Lavandula are small evergreen bushy plants with narrow spiked flowers. These types of lavender are popularly referred to as English lavender and are prized for their fragrance. Although they like full sun, they can survive in most climates (even the distinctly un-sunny British Isles) in well-drained soil. They produce classic purple flowers and silvery grey leaves.

Bract Lavenders

Bract lavenders are colourful dwarf lavenders in purple and deep red with bracts, or ears. The flowers look like butterflies and often grow wild in Mediterranean countries. They were traditionally grown for their fragrance and insect-repellent properties. They are also known as French lavender (*Lavandula stoechas, see* page 18) but they grow in Spain (where they are predictably known as Spanish lavender) and other Mediterranean countries. They are tender and need to be grown in pots in cold climates so they can overwinter in a greenhouse.

English Lavenders in Depth

The Best of English

English lavender is the popular name for *Lavandula angustifolia* and there are several different types of lavender within this family of plants. When you're buying English lavender from a garden centre, mail-order catalogue or online it can be difficult to decide which to plump for. Here are some of our favourites – we think you'll love them too.

Lavandula angustifolia 'Loddon Pink' AGM

Commonly known as English lavender Loddon Pink, these plants have dusky pink fragrant flowers, green/silver leaves and are bushy and compact. They need a well-drained sheltered sunny spot to thrive.

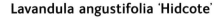

Lavandula angustifolia 'Hidcote'

This is a bushy purple dwarf evergreen lavender. It has silvery–grey leaves and deep purple flowers in aromatic spikes 3–4 cm in length. It can survive below–zero temperatures, and can grow to a height and spread of 0.1–0.5 m (4–20 in) in a two–to–five–year period. It is best grown in full sun in well–drained soil and in a sheltered position, and makes a great hedge.

Munstead

This variety is named after the plants grown at the garden of the famous gardener Gertrude Jekyll at Munstead Woods, Godalming in Surrey, England, in the late nineteenth and early twentieth centuries. Munstead produces dense spikes of perfumed blue–purple flowers from July to September and grey–green leaves.

Rosea

This type of lavender bears dark rose pink flowers and has steely grey–green leaves. It looks good grown alongside roses and is hardy.

Alba

These are frost–hardy evergreen compact lavenders with grey–green leaves and scented white flowers. Like the others in the *Lavandula angustifolia* family, they thrive in full sun.

French Lavenders in Depth

Vive le Difference

French lavender, or *Lavandula stoechas*, is more flamboyant than English lavender varieties with distinctive colourful bracts, or ears. They produce dark purple and pink and deep red flowers, but are less hardy than their English cousins.

Lavandula stoechas (French Lavender)

These plants have a camphor scent, deep purple flowers topped with a mauve bract. They have a long flowering period from late spring to early autumn, but require protection from frost.

Lavandula stoechas 'Kew Red'

This plant has tender, red flowers topped with pale pink bracts. They flower from late spring to early autumn, but need protection from wet winters.

Lavandula stoechas 'Helmsdale'

This type originates from New Zealand and has camphor-scented grey-green leaves and deep reddish-purple flowers with burgundy bracts. They have a distinctive scent and grow to a height of 0.6 m (2 ft).

Lavandula stoechas subsp. Pedunculata

This lavender has small round purple flower heads tipped with large purple bracts. It will grow in a warm, sunny position, in well-drained soil and grows well by the seaside. The flowers are highly scented and it should grow to 1 m (3¼ ft) in height and width.

Lavandula latifolia

This type of lavender is easy to grow in a hot climate; it hates waterlogged soil. It also has a high oil yield so is popular with commercial growers, but because the oil has a camphor/menthol smell, it is less valuable than sweeter-smelling English lavender oil.

Lavandula × intermedia

Lavandula × intermedia is a hybrid of English and Portuguese lavenders. They combine the hardiness of an English lavender with the heat tolerance of the Portuguese/spike lavender. They have a high flower yield and a strong scent – the best of both worlds – making them popular with commercial growers and home gardeners alike.

Grosso

Lavandula × latifolia grosso is the primary commercial variety for production of lavender oil and one of the best all-round lavender performers. It has strong large violet-blue flowers, silver/grey foliage, long wand-like flower stems and is highly aromatic. It can grow to 0.6-0.8 m (2–2½ ft) in height and spread.

A History of Lavender

Lavender has been mentioned throughout history over thousands of years for its medicinal and culinary uses. The Egyptians were using it to embalm bodies in the days of the pharaohs, and the Romans used it for bathing, cooking and scenting the air. Every great civilization seems to have developed a use for it.

Origins

The Healing Herb

Over the centuries it has been consistently hailed as a miracle all-purpose herb. The Greek physician Dioscorides (c. 40–90 AD) recommended lavender as a tea-like infusion for congested breathing and chest complaints. Pliny the Elder used it to treat the 'distressing symptoms of bereavement', and in the Middle Ages it became a must-have for most monastery herb gardens and medicine chests.

The Mediterranean

Lavender is thought to have originated in the Mediterranean, spreading across Europe from Greece, reaching France by around 600 BC. It is mentioned in the Bible (referred to as 'spikenard'), and Mary used lavender oil to anoint Jesus after the crucifixion. By the Middle Ages, lavender was being used across Europe in laundry.

Lavender Reaches England

One of the first mentions of lavender being grown in England is in 1301, in the records of Merton Priory, although it is highly likely the Romans cultivated it when they colonized Britain from the first century AD.

After Henry VIII dissolved the monasteries (1536–41), lavender started being grown in domestic gardens. Lavender bushes would be planted near laundry rooms so that clothes could be laid on them to scent them.

Lavender and Royalty

Royalty seems to have had a love affair with lavender over the centuries. The Queen of Sheba sent lavender oil to King Solomon as a gift. Queen Elizabeth I of England requested lavender conserve to be served at her table every day. She is also thought to have used it for migraines. Charles VI of France loved lavender–filled pillows to help him sleep, and King Louis XIV took a fancy to bathing in lavender–scented bath water. Queen Victoria was the real royal lavender devotee – she made it fashionable and had it dried and made into muslin sachets to hang in wardrobes and use in linen presses.

Lavender in the Great Plague

During the Great Plague of London (1664–66) lavender was tied around the wrists to ward off infection. It is widely credited as an ingredient of the posies mentioned in the children's nursery rhyme *Ring a Ring o' Roses*, which is believed to describe how people fell down dead during the Great Plague.

Lavender is For Love

Lavender has also gained a reputation for being the herb of love – not because it is an aphrodisiac, but probably more likely because it induces deep relaxation. Cleopatra is said to have used lavender's scent to seduce Julius Caesar and Mark Antony.

Grown in Every Garden

By the seventeenth century lavender was so well established in England that the famous herbalist Nicholas Culpeper wrote, 'lavender was an inhabitant almost in every garden, it is so well known it needs no description'.

London's Lavender Fields

By the nineteenth century, the London suburbs of Mitcham and Carshalton became the centre of the booming English lavender industry. The lavender was picked and distilled to extract the oil and this was used to make toiletries and medicines, as well as skin and haircare products.

Lavender in Hospitals

Florence Nightingale, the founder of modern nursing, was reported to have anointed the foreheads of wounded soldiers with lavender oil during the Crimean War to help them relax. She was following in the tradition of Roman soldiers, who are said to have used lavender oil to heal their wounds.

Lavender on the Battlefield

By the time of the First World War, diluted lavender oil was being used to disinfect floors in hospitals and speed up the healing of wounds, minimizing the risk of infection. However, after the introduction of penicillin in the 1940s, the use of lavender oil in mainstream medicine declined for several decades.

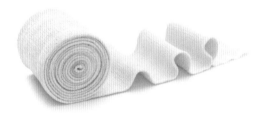

Lavender and Aromatherapy

In the 1940s in France a renaissance occurred in the use of lavender oil in aromatherapy, after some chance discoveries by doctors. Gattefosse, a French chemist, burned his hand and arm so badly that gangrene set in. Rather than amputate – the only treatment available at the time – he treated it with essential oil of lavender and it quickly healed. He was so impressed that he dedicated his life to the use of essential oils for skin problems.

The Essential Oil Boom

Lavender essential oil has enjoyed a revival in popularity in recent years as its use in complementary medicine has increased. Lavender oil is now one of the widely used essential oils and is used in massage as a relaxant and mood booster, as well as treating scar tissue. Visit any chemist or supermarket and you'll find scores of cosmetic, herbal remedies and cleaning products made with lavender essential oil.

Super Bugs

These days lavender essential oil's antibacterial properties are widely recognized – particularly in the fight against so-called super bugs, which have become resistant to broad-spectrum antibiotics.

Cultivation

Travels Well

In the United States and Canada, the Shakers – or the United Society of Believers in Christ's Second Appearing – were the first to grow lavender commercially in herb gardens to make herbal remedies in the 1600s. The farming of lavender rapidly spread across the world. For example, in 1921 Mr and Mrs Denny emigrated from Devon to Tasmania with lavender seeds from the French Alps and established Bridestowe, a successful lavender farm which survives to this day.

Easy to Grow

The best time to plant lavender is in the spring. It doesn't need rich soil; in fact it thrives in poor or moderately fertile, free-draining alkaline soil. It requires fairly little maintenance, making it a fantastic addition to your garden with no fuss required.

Availability

That Wonderful Smell

The smell of lavender must now be one of the most familiar scents in the world and has never really gone out of fashion. Although it can't be grown in all climates, the scent is familiar to people all over the planet. You can see it growing on the heady purple hilltops of Provence or enjoy the fragrance as you pass an inner-city roundabout planted by guerilla gardening groups.

Where Is Lavender Grown Today?

Provence in the south of France is the picturesque home of lavender oil production. But it is also now grown and distilled in bigger farms in Bulgaria, Ukraine, the former Yugoslavia, Czech Republic, southern Russia, Australia and China. It is also grown in South Africa and New Zealand as well as the US, Canada and the UK.

Laundry & Cleaning

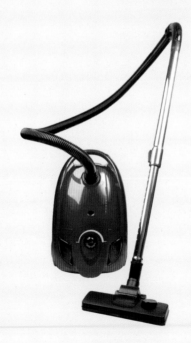

Laundry

Lavender's fresh, summery scent is preferred by many as an alternative to the more clinical smell of some commercial cleaning agents, and for more than a few the scent evokes old memories. Lavender essential oil or dried lavender from your garden can make dozens of different cleaning products – the following pages will tell you how.

Washing Your Clothes

Old Lavender Lore

There's nothing new about using lavender in laundry. As far back as Elizabethan times clothes were laid out on lavender bushes to perfume them. It was the Victorian poet John Keats who wrote:

> 'And still she slept an azure-lidded sleep,
> In blanched linen, smooth, and lavender'd'.

Putting on clothes that feel clean and smell fresh gets your day off to a feel-good start. Put some natural cleaning power in your wash by adding lavender essential oil.

A Modern Alternative

If you find today's washing powders harsh and expensive, try making your own lavender–scented blend – at a fraction of the price. Boil 300 ml/½ pint/1 cups water in a pan, then add a grated bar of castile soap and stir until the soap dissolves. Allow the mixture to cool slightly and then add 125 g/ 4 oz/½ cup borax and 10 drops lavender essential oil and mix well. Do this outdoors or wear a mask to avoid breathing it in.

Lavender, Lemon and Cloves Detergent

Grate a bar of natural soap (such as olive oil) and then mix the soap flakes with 1 litre/1¾ pints/ 4 cups hot boiled water in a saucepan and stir until the soap melts. Then add the mix to a 5–gallon bucket half–filled with hot water, together with 200 g/7 oz/1 cup washing soda (sodium carbonate) and 50 g/2 oz/¼ cup borax. Stir until all the powder is dissolved and leave overnight. In the morning add 30 drops lavender essential oil, 30 drops lemon essential oil and 30 drops clove oil.

The liquid can be stored in plastic containers. Shake before use to disperse lumps and use ½ cup per wash. Makes enough detergent for 90 machine washes.

Wash For Delicates

For delicate hand washing, mix together 4 tablespoons grated castile soap, 8 tablespoons sodium lauryl sulphate and ¼ teaspoon lavender essential oil. Dissolve 1 tablespoon of the powder in a sink of warm water.

Removing Stains

Add dried lavender and a lemon slice to 250 ml/8 fl oz/1 cup water and boil. Strain the water and then mix with 100 g/7 oz/1 cup bicarbonate of soda (baking soda), 500 ml/18 fl oz/2 cups clear washing-up liquid and 500 ml/18 fl oz/2 cups hydrogen peroxide. Pour into a spray bottle and spray onto stains. Leave for a few hours and then wash as normal.

Deodorizing

If your clothes smell dank and musty or are stained with body odour, you can banish unpleasant smells by adding 10–15 lavender essential oil drops to your washing liquid.

Disinfecting

If for whatever reason you need to disinfect clothes – after your child has vomited on sheets for instance – try rinsing the sheets and then soaking in a sink or bucket of water and add 2 capfuls lavender essential oil for 30–40 minutes before machine washing.

CAUTION: Lavender can cause skin irritation. Discontinue use if you notice any redness.

Conditioning Your Clothes

Lavender Tumble Dryer Bags

Try adding a cotton/muslin bag filled with dried lavender flowers to your tumble dryer. An alternative is to put several drops lavender essential oil on a clean, lint-free rag or washcloth and add to a dryer-load of clothes at the beginning of the cycle.

Fabric Softener

Mix white vinegar with lavender essential oil and use in place of or in addition to commercial fabric softener, adding the mix to the tray of your washing machine.

Feng Shui Your Clothes

Lavender is considered an ancient symbol of love and cleanliness and can be used to wash and freshen clothes and scent clothes hanging in wardrobes. Feng Shui practitioners sometimes burn lavender sticks to shift negative stagnant energy in a home and create a feeling of space.

Linen Cupboard

Store your sheets in a linen cupboard with lavender sachets on each shelf. The aroma will penetrate the linen and smell sweet when you make up your bed – the aroma may even help you sleep. Lavender will also help repel moths and silver fish.

Aftercare For Your Clothes

Lavender Ironing Spray

Another way to fragrance your clothes is to spritz them with lavender water. Mix 1 teaspoon/4 drops lavender essential oil with 50 ml/2 fl oz/¼ cup vodka and then pour into a clean spray bottle and add 900 ml/1½ pints/ 3¾ cups water and shake. You can make this without the vodka, but you'll have to shake the bottle harder to get the oil to separate from the water.

Banish Smelly Shoes

If stinky shoes are a problem, put a cotton wool ball dabbed with lavender essential oil in the shoes to freshen them up.

Make Lavender-scented Drawer Liners

Take some wrapping paper and cut it to fit the drawer you are lining. Then mix up 2 parts water to 1 part lavender essential oil, dip a cotton wool ball in the mixture and dab onto the back of the paper. Allow to thoroughly dry and then place in the drawer.

Kitchen & Bathroom

Lavender is a natural antiseptic and antibacterial agent and is a useful ingredient for home-made cleaning products. Even in commercial factory-made cleaning products, lavender is often added to cleaning agents as it masks the 'chemical' smell of the agents. Studies by scientists have confirmed that lavender oil does have antibacterial properties: a Chinese research study in 2010 revealed lavender essential oil was active against some of the most potent forms of bacteria.

Kitchen Items & Surfaces

Kitchen Counters

Keeping kitchen counters scrupulously clean is vital in preventing bugs such as *Escherichia coli* (commonly referred to as *E. coli*), a species of bacteria commonly found in the intestines of humans and animals, which can cause diarrhoea. Recent research has confirmed lavender oil has an antibacterial effect on *E. coli*.

There are lots of variations on home-made spray recipes, but combining lavender oil with tea tree oil, which also has strong antibacterial properties, and water is a particularly powerful cleaning cocktail. Take a clean spray bottle and add 250 ml/8 fl oz/1 cup water with ¼ teaspoon lavender essential oil and ¼ teaspoon tea tree oil. Shake and squirt.

CAUTION: Always patch test home-made cleaning agents to check it won't damage your work surfaces – particularly granite, limestone and marble.

Disinfect Cleaning Cloths

Soak your cleaning cloths in the lavender tea tree solution to disinfect them and avoid cross-contamination, and change them regularly as they can harbour bacteria.

Deep Clean Your Chopping Boards

Chopping boards are a common cause of cross-contamination. For instance, if you have prepared raw meat on a chopping board and then use it to prepare other uncooked food, you run the risk of picking up bugs such as *E. coli* and Campylobacter, a bacterium found in raw poultry, which can cause diarrhoea.

As a general rule, use different chopping boards for meat and for raw foods such as vegetables to avoid cross-contamination.

You should also sterilize boards after use. Try using a lavender oil-based disinfectant. Mix 20 drops of lavender essential oil in a cup of water.

Stove Top Cleaning

You can wipe down your stove top with a lavender disinfectant (*see* opposite), but for more stubborn stains you can also make up a paste with 75 g/ 2²⁄₃ oz/¹⁄₃ cup bicarbonate soda (baking soda) so that you get a nice moist paste. Put the paste on a sponge or brush and scrub away.

CAUTION: Always patch test first to check the mixture doesn't damage your stove top.

Kitchen Sink

To clean and disinfect your sink, use the spray mix recipe (*see* page 39) to give your sink a good coating. Then wipe with a cloth, or if the sink needs a really good clean, a sponge with a scrubbing surface on the back.

If your sink has a greasy residue, put the plug in, give it a good scrub with the sponge, then put enough hot water in to cover the greasy area. Add washing–up liquid and 5–6 drops lavender oil. Leave to soak for a while, then empty the water out and clean with a sponge.

CAUTION: Always patch test ceramic sinks to avoid causing any damage.

Kitchen Table

In our haste to clear away, the kitchen table is sometimes only given a cursory wipe – but like a kitchen worktop it can also harbour bacteria, which can linger and quickly colonize the area. Get into the habit of wiping your kitchen table after every meal with a lavender and water cleaning spray (*see* page 40).

Microwave Cleaning

Odours can linger in microwaves. Try this paste recipe to banish them and make it smell fresh again. Mix up 50 g/2 oz/¼ cup bicarbonate of soda (baking soda) with 1 teaspoon white vinegar and add 5 drops lavender oil to make a paste. Apply it to the interior door of the microwave. Leave for 15 minutes and then wipe off.

Wipe Out Your Fridge

Because lavender oil has disinfecting and antiseptic properties, it's a helpful weapon in the fight against mould. You don't need very much, just 250 ml/8 fl oz/1 cup hot water with a few drops of lavender oil in it. Dampen a clean cloth with the water mixture and wipe down the inside of your fridge – and any other parts where you have a mould problem. Wipe out with a clean cloth to avoid odour clinging to foods.

Freshen Up Your Dishwasher

The dishwasher is a kitchen work–horse that can be overlooked in your everyday cleaning – but food debris odour can start to smell if left to build up. Clean and freshen it up with a good wipe-down with lavender oil wash. Mix 250 ml/8 fl oz/1 cup hot water with a few drops of lavender oil in it and give the inside and outside of your dishwasher a thorough wipe. If there's any dishwasher soap that won't come off, wipe it off with some lavender oil on a damp cloth. Wipe it all again with fresh water afterwards to avoid your crockery tasting of lavender.

Disinfect Your Bin

Nasty smells caused by chemicals given off by decomposing food can linger in your kitchen bin. Get into the routine off rinsing it out at least once a week. Remove the bag and add the contents of a bucket of hot water with a few drops of lavender and tea tree oils and some washing–up liquid. Leave for 10 minutes and then empty, wiping dry with a kitchen towel.

Fragrance Your Floors

Mop your floors with hot water and a few drops of lavender oil and some washing–up liquid for a fragrant once over. The lavender oil will also disinfect the floor surface, keeping it free of bugs.

CAUTION: Always patch test on floors.

Stench Buster

If you cook curries, garlic dishes, fish or fried food the odours can linger. Make up your own kitchen room spray by filling a plastic bottle with a spray dispenser with water and adding 8 drops lavender oil, 10 drops eucalyptus and 5 drops lemongrass.

Kitchen Cupboards

The packets of food that we keep in our kitchen cupboards can attract insects. Lavender has a strong insect–repelling effect. Give your cupboards a good wipe regularly with a mixture of 1 cup hot water with a few drops of lavender oil added to it. This should keep those uninvited guests away. It will also give your cupboards a clean, fresh scent.

Tackle Greasy Wall Tiles

Oil from cooking can leave a greasy film on wall tiles – particularly above stove tops. Make up a container of 50 per cent water and 50 per cent white vinegar and add 5 drops lavender oil and shake. A white vinegar spray should dissolve greasy marks. Spray on and wipe off.

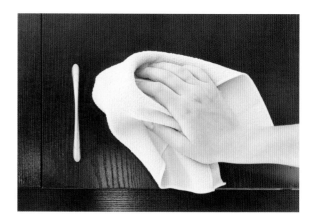

Bathroom

Floor Cleaner

The bathroom is one of those really important areas of the home where the floor needs to be immaculately clean to stop the spread of bacteria. If your bathroom floor is a hard surface you can clean it really well using warm water with a small amount of lavender oil in it (2 teaspoons lavender oil to half a bucket of warm water).

Remove Tile Mould

If the tiles around your bath or shower are looking grubby, try making up a paste with the following ingredients. First mix 3 parts bicarbonate of soda (baking soda)

with 1 part castile soap and 5 drops lavender essential oil, and add enough water to make a paste. Apply the paste to the affected areas and scrub with an old toothbrush before rinsing.

Banish Bathroom Mildew

If you get mould build-up in the shower or on the bathroom windowsill, try the following two-stage approach. Make up a disinfectant by combining 50 g/4 oz/¼ cup borax with 500 ml/18 fl oz/2 cups hot water and 10 drops tea tree oil. Spray on and let it work in for a few minutes and then rinse off. Then apply a mixture of 4 parts water to 2 parts vinegar and add 5 drops each lavender and tea tree oil (both have antifungal properties) and wipe off.

Soap Scum Scourer

If your sink or bath has soap scum build-up, add 1 tablespoon bicarbonate of soda (baking soda), 1 teaspoon salt, 2 drops lavender essential oil and just enough white vinegar to make a paste. Scrub the sink or bath and rinse well and leave a little vinegar on it overnight to remove any remaining residue.

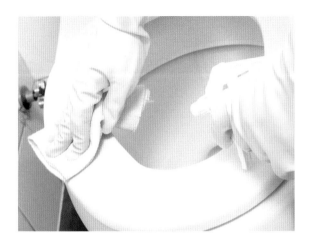

Toilet Bowl Cleaning

Toilets are a breeding ground for nasty bacteria. Keep the bugs at bay by mixing up 150 g/5 oz/³⁄₄ cup bicarbonate of soda (baking soda) with 120 ml/4 fl oz/1/2 cup water. Add ½ teaspoon liquid castile soap, 5 drops tea tree oil and 5 drops lavender oil. Squirt around the toilet bowl, including under the rim and also the toilet seat.

Toilet Scrub For Stubborn Stains

If you have a ring around the toilet bowl mix 10 drops lavender oil with 200 g/7 oz/1 cup borax and 250 ml/8 fl oz/1 cup white vinegar and 5 drops tea tree oil. Then leave in the toilet overnight and clean with a toilet brush and flush away next day.

Disinfectant Spray

Cleaning products such as bleach can be harsh and sometime trigger chemical sensitivities in people. Try a natural disinfectant by combining 5 drops lavender oil with water and 5 drops eucalyptus oil. Fill a spray bottle with water and add oils. Shake well before use.

General Household Cleaning

Lavender oil can give your home a well-tended sparkling appearance without the cloying fumes of chemicals. Mixed with beeswax, lavender oil makes rich wooden furniture polish; added to water it can clean floors; and mixed with vinegar it leaves your windows gleaming. Even adding lavender to a vacuum cleaner can help banish stale odours from carpets and upholstery. Many of the lavender-based home-cleaning products on the following pages have the added bonus of being simple and inexpensive to make.

Cleaning Wood and Windows

Polishing Wood

Cleaning your wooden furniture and floors with lavender furniture polish gives your home a sweet fragrance that lasts, while protecting its natural beauty. Lavender and beeswax has been a popular furniture polish for centuries. You can make your own lavender polish by mixing 30 g/1 oz yellow beeswax with 120 ml/4 fl oz/½ cup turpentine and 15 drops lavender essential oil. Grate beeswax with a cheese grater and then heat in a basin over a pan of simmering water until completely melted. Remove from the heat and stir in the turpentine before the wax goes hard. Store in a glass pot with a resealable lid.

Apply the wax in a thin layer with a soft cloth and buff it up. Waxes offer the simplest of finishes for wooden surfaces, while feeding and protecting it too.

CAUTION: Do not add the turpentine while the wax is being heated, as it is flammable – add as the wax cools after it is removed from the heat.

Lavender Oil For Cleaning Windows

Chemical window cleaners are expensive and leave a strong odour and sometimes messy streaks too. Making your own cleaner is cheaper, smells great and is more environmentally friendly.

Add 300 ml/$\frac{1}{2}$ pint/1$\frac{1}{4}$ cups distilled water to 150 ml/$\frac{1}{4}$ pint/ $\frac{2}{3}$ cup white vinegar and combine with 5 drops each of lemon and lavender essential oils. Pour into a spray bottle and then shake. Spray onto glass and then remove with a clean cloth or sheet of kitchen paper.

Tackle Streaky Windows

Sometimes windows can be streaked with the hard-to-shift build-up from commercial cleaning agents and grime. Get rid of dirty streaks with the following recipe. Combine 120 ml/4 fl oz/$\frac{1}{2}$ cup each of surgical spirit (rubbing alcohol) and water with $\frac{1}{4}$ teaspoon liquid dishwasher in a spray bottle. Add 5 drops lemon, tea tree or lavender essential oil. Shake well.

Heavy-Duty Window Cleaner

This is a slightly stronger version of the recipe opposite, formulated to tackle the most stubborn build-up. Mix together 250 ml/8 fl oz/1 cup each water and white vinegar or vodka with ¼ teaspoon liquid dishwasher soap in a spray bottle. Add 5 drops lavender essential oil. Shake well. To apply it, spray on and then wipe off with clean cloth.

Lavender and Peppermint Glass Cleaner

Try this variation on the above recipe for a more pungent-smelling cleaning liquid. Combine 250 ml/8 fl oz/1 cup vinegar with 120 ml/ 4 fl oz/½ cup water, 10 drops lavender oil, and 5 drops peppermint oil. Place in a plastic bottle with a spray dispenser and shake to mix.

Useful Window Cleaning Tips

Try washing your windows on a cloudy day and not in direct sunlight – streaks are caused by the cleaning solution drying too quickly. Also, newspaper is an old-fashioned (and free) material for cleaning windows.

Room Fragrances

Clean Smells

Home–made sprays are useful for freshening up bathrooms, kitchens, bedrooms and living rooms, adding a clean but calming fragrance.

To make a general room freshener, try filling a plastic spray bottle with 250 ml/8 fl oz/1 cup water and add 6 drops lavender oil, 4 drops peppermint and 5 drops clary sage.

Feeling a bit stressed after a hard day's work? Try this air freshener mixture for helping relieve anxiety after a stressful day. Pour 250 ml/8 fl oz /1 cup distilled water into a spray bottle and add 4 drops lavender oil and 3 drops rose essential oil. Shake before use.

Another mixture you can make works great as a bedtime spritzer. Add 4 drops lavender oil and 3 drops chamomile essential oil to 250 ml/8 fl oz /1 cup distilled water and pour into a plastic bottle. Spray your bedroom half an hour before bedtime for a calming and relaxing atmosphere.

Using a Fragrance Diffuser

Another way of enjoying the fragrance of lavender at home is by using a diffuser – a ceramic burner with a space for a tea light underneath a dish where diluted essential oils can be warmed.

Mix together 8–10 drops lavender essential oil, with 2–3 drops palmarosa essential oil and 2–3 drops rose/geranium oil and heat in a burner to create a calming atmosphere.

Relaxing Lavender and Cedarwood Blend

This is a perfect blend for relaxing and chilling out at home. Blend together 4 drops lavender essential oil, 2 drops cedarwood essential oil and 2 drops orange essential oil.

Sick Room Disinfectant

Burn 8 drops lavender essential oil in a diffuser to help disinfect a sick room and relax the patient – lavender oil has antibacterial and antiviral properties and has also been shown to induce relaxation and sleep.

CAUTION: Never leave oil burners or diffusers unattended.

Deodorizing

Freshen Up Your Carpets

Carpets feel luxurious and cosy underfoot but dirt can get ingrained and make them smell stale and musty. Try deodorizing your carpet by mixing up 40 drops essential oils (15 drops lavender, 10 drops clove and 15 drops orange), with 200 g/7 oz/1 cup bicarbonate of soda (baking soda) in a plastic freezer bag. Seal and leave for 24 hours and then sprinkle on your carpets an hour before vacuuming. Always patch test first.

Dried Lavender Carpet Freshener

You can also combine 1.3 kg/3 lb/6 cups bicarbonate of soda (baking soda) with 3 cups dried lavender flowers and 130 g/4½ oz/1 cup cornstarch (cornflour) in a sealed plastic container. Leave for a few days and then sprinkle onto the carpets and leave for an hour before vacuuming.

CAUTION: Always patch test on a corner of the carpet which can be covered by furniture.

Perfume Power From Your Vacuum

Perhaps one of the simplest tips for freshening up your carpets quickly is to slip a few drops of lavender essential oil into your vacuum bag or filter.

You can also make up a muslin square or section of knotted tights filled with a handful of dried lavender and rosemary, 1 tablespoon cloves, 1 tablespoon bicarbonate of soda (baking soda) and 5–7 drops lavender oil. Store the mixture in a sealed container for 1 week and then add 3 tablespoons to each muslin/nylon pouch and either stitch or tie shut before placing in the vacuum bag. It's less messy than applying mixtures directly to the carpet.

Curtains and Upholstery

Fill a spray bottle with water and add 4–5 drops lavender essential oil. Swirl the spray bottle around to mix the oil with the water, then spray over your curtains and upholstery to freshen them up.

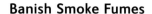

Banish Smoke Fumes

To banish cigarette smoke odours, sprinkle your carpet with bicarbonate of soda (baking soda), using as much as is needed to cover the size of the room and top with dried lavender flowers. Leave for at least 5 hours and vacuum.

Burnt Food

To remove the odour of burnt food, follow the cigarette smoke recipe above and then pour white vinegar into bowls and leave around the room for 3–5 days.

Pet Smells

Freshen up your home and the dog's blanket or basket by making up a liquid spray. Add 6 drops each of essential lavender, orange, peppermint, eucalyptus and tea tree oils to a plastic bottle of water and shake to mix.

CAUTION: Do not use essential oils on cats (*see* page 119).

General Cleaning Tips

Scent Some Pine Cones

Try soaking some pine cones in 150 ml/¼
pint/⅔ cup water with 25 drops lavender oil
overnight and allow to dry. Keep away from
fire as they are highly flammable.

Polish Your Floors

Make your wooden floors clean and hygienic by washing them with a disinfecting water and
lavender oil solution. Add 2 teaspoons to half a bucket of water and mop your floor as normal.

Tackling Problem Areas

Tackle a smelly nappy (diaper) bin by regularly rinsing it out with a solution of lavender oil,
simultaneously disinfecting and making fragrant. Another tip is to put a baby wipe soaked in
lavender oil in the bottom of the bin.

Streak-Free Mirrors

Give your mirrors a good spring clean with your homemade cleanser. Put 250 ml/8 fl oz/
1 cup white vinegar and 5 drops lavender oil into a spray bottle. Spray and wipe dry with
a soft cloth.

Personal Care

Appearance

Lavender has been used as an ingredient in beauty products by everyone from Cleopatra to Queen Victoria, Marilyn Monroe to Queen Elizabeth II. The plant is well known for its calming, soothing properties, which make it a useful natural ingredient for skin products. It is also used in haircare products and as a perfume. Some types of lavender can be used in products to treat head lice or make insect repellents.

Oral Hygiene

Lavender Mouthwash

Lavender is an obvious ingredient for mouthwash for its antibacterial qualities and sweet smell. Boil enough water to make several cups of mouthwash and pour into a teapot. Then add a tea strainer filled with 2 teaspoons of dried lavender flowers and soak for 10 minutes before removing. Allow to cool and transfer into a plastic bottle and chill in the fridge and then use to rinse your mouth after brushing your teeth.

CAUTION: Use in small amounts to check for any sensitivity and if you are taking any prescription drugs check with your doctor for any drug interactions.

Did You Know?

Along with other herbs, lavender is also used as an ingredient in some toothpastes formulated to help fight gum disease. Research published in the *African Journal of Microbial Research* shows that lavender oil destroys several types of bacteria.

Lavender and Bad Breath

Scientists at the Hebrew University in Jerusalem are currently investigating whether a patch containing lavender, echinachea and sage can neutralize the chemical compound released by the bacteria that cause bad breath.

Skincare

Greasy Skin And Acne

Lavender oil's astringent, antiseptic and antibacterial properties mean that it is often included in treatments for skin conditions. Acne is a common skin condition affecting around 80 per cent of 11 to 30 year olds; it causes blackheads, white heads and spots. The key to controlling it is keeping your skin clean, so cleaning it twice a day with a lavender-based product may help and may also reduce redness by calming inflammation.

Steam Clean

A great way to open blocked pores is through steaming your face by adding a few drops lavender oil to a bowl hot water. Clean any make-up off your face and then inhale the steam for around 15 minutes. It will not only benefit your skin but it's a great way to help you wind down too.

Acne Gel

An alternative method is to make a cool lavender and tea tree acne gel. Chop 20 lavender flower heads, 10 rose geranium flowers and leaves, 8 marigold flowers and cover with 200 ml/7 fl oz/¾ cup boiled water, leaving it to steep for 10 minutes. Place in a blender and strain the mixture through a muslin cloth into a bowl. In another bowl dissolve a sachet of vegetable gelatine in 2 tablespoons cold water. Add the flower infusion gradually and then 5 teaspoons vodka and 20 drops tea tree oil, so you get a gel consistency. Store in a pot with a pump dispenser. It keeps in the fridge for up to 6 weeks.

DIY Lavender Skin Tonic

You can apply this neat to the skin if you have inflamed acne or use it diluted as an astringent to tone open pores. Cover fresh lavender flower heads with white wine vinegar. Store somewhere cold and dark and shake the mixture daily. After a week you can strain it with a muslin cloth into a jar and it's ready to use.

Face Scrub

This is a great exfoliator to remove dead skin cells and give you a fresh complexion. Grind 15 g/½ oz/½ cup lavender flowers and mix with 50 g/2 oz/ ½ cup ground unsalted almonds and 100 g/4 oz/1 cup ground oatmeal. Apply the paste to your face with warm water using a circular motion, leave for 5 minutes and rinse off.

You can also use it for removing dry skin on problem areas such as the elbows and bottoms of your feet.

Acne Face Mask

 This face pack may help to soothe acne. Warm 1 teaspoon honey and add 5 drops lavender oil, ½ teaspoon minced garlic, ½ teaspoon sugar and enough milk to produce a spreading consistency. Apply and leave for 10–15 minutes before rinsing off.

CAUTION: Always patch test any mixtures before applying to the skin.

The Queen of Hungary's Water

Allegedly invented by the Queen of Hungary (although the history is admittedly a little vague on this!), this is a popular gypsy remedy. It can also be used as an eau de cologne (and as a bonus, also as a hair tonic for greasy hair).

There are various recipes but try this combination – 6 tablespoons lemon balm leaves, 4 tablespoons rose petals, peel of 1 lemon, 4 tablespoons chamomile leaves, 3 tablespoons calendula flowers, 1 tablespoon lemon zest, 1 tablespoon dried rosemary and 1 tablespoon dried sage.

Place all the herbs and flowers in a large jar with enough cider vinegar or vodka to cover. Seal and store in a cool, dark place, shaking every day. After 2 weeks strain the mixture with a muslin cloth to remove all the herbs and add 3 drops lavender essential oil. Store in a sealed jar for up to 12 months, but keep in the dark as heat and light will damage the liquid.

Cleanser and Moisturizer

This is a delicious-smelling moisturizer to nourish your skin and can be used as a make-up remover. Take 1 tablespoon aloe vera gel and blend with 100 ml/ 3½ fl oz/⅓ cup olive oil. Set aside. In the microwave melt 1 tablespoon white beeswax for 30 seconds.

Then mix together the olive oil/aloe vera mix and the beeswax. Add 2 tablespoons rosewater and 2–3 drops lavender essential oil, stirring until the mixture reaches a creamy consistency. Pour into a jar and seal with a lid.

Hand Cream

Make a nourishing hand cream by melting 4 tablespoons beeswax with 2 tablespoons shea butter, and then add 10 drops lavender essential oil and 8 tablespoons evening primrose oil. Mix until a smooth consistency is reached and pour into a jar to set.

Lavender And Lemon Toner

Lavender is well known for its astringent effects, so great for tightening open pores. Try mixing 2 drops lavender water with 3 drops lemon oil and 3 teaspoons distilled water and apply with cotton wool.

CAUTION: Always patch test any cosmetic recipes on your skin.

Lavender and Rosemary Face Cream

This is a great moisturizer for combination/oily skin prone to spots. First melt 1 teaspoon beeswax, 2 teaspoons cocoa butter and 4 tablespoons jojoba oil in a stainless steel bowl in a saucepan of water. In a second pan heat some water and melt 4 teaspoons vegetable emulsifying wax with 2 tablespoons lavender infusion (made by steeping fresh lavender flowers in boiling water for 10 minutes) in a stainless steel bowl. When melted, quickly whisk and add 5 drops each lavender, rosemary and chamomile essential oils. Pour into a dark–coloured jar.

Lavender Ointment

Melt 75 g/3 oz beeswax and 25 g/1 oz cocoa butter and add 25–30 drops lavender essential oil, 150 ml/$\frac{1}{3}$ pint/$\frac{2}{3}$ cup sweet almond oil and 15 drops vitamin E oil. Pour the mixture into a container and seal.

Lavender Foot Soak

If you've got tired, aching feet, try this relaxing foot soak for some effortless revival. Fill a bucket with hot water, add 65 g/2$\frac{1}{2}$ oz/$\frac{1}{4}$ cup Epsom salts, 15 g/$\frac{1}{2}$ oz/$\frac{1}{4}$ cup rosemary leaves and 3 drops lavender essential oil.

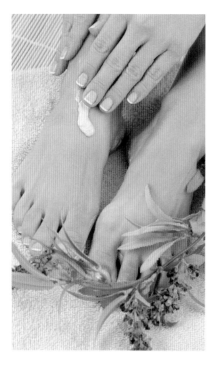

Foot Reviving Balm

Dry your feet after the foot soak above and then spoil them with this reviving foot balm. Melt 12 g/$\frac{1}{2}$ oz beeswax and 2 tablespoons cocoa butter and remove from the heat. After cooling, add 5 drops each lavender, peppermint and tea tree oils, plus $\frac{3}{4}$ tablespoon vegetable glycerine, 50 ml/2 fl oz/$\frac{1}{4}$ cup sweet almond oil, 50 ml/2 fl oz/$\frac{1}{4}$ cup apricot kernel oil and 2 tablespoons jojoba oil. Then pour into a container.

Lavender Foot Scrub

For a revitalizing foot scrub try the following. Melt 4 tablespoons cocoa butter with 4 tablespoons jojoba oil in a microwave. Remove from heat and then add 8 drops lavender essential oil and 50 g/2 oz/$\frac{1}{3}$ cup Epsom salts.

Treating Cold Sores

Cold sores are small, unsightly and sometimes painful blisters that develop on the lips or around the mouth. They are caused by the herpes simplex virus and usually clear up without treatment within 7–10 days. The virus stays in your body permanently, and cold sore outbreaks can be triggered by stress, exposure to sun/wind, a low immune system, fever or other viral infections.

Dabbing neat lavender essential oil on some cotton wool and applying to the cold sore may shorten its duration – particularly if you catch it early.

Insect Repellent

To protect yourself from annoying mosquitoes, add a few drops lavender oil to a teaspoon of carrier oil and apply to your skin. Lavender contains geraniol, a compound also found in geraniums that repels insects.

CAUTION: Lavender oil can increase photosensitivity if used in sunlight, so stay in the shade if applying it.

Lovely Lip Balm

Treat your lips to some lavender lip balm. Gently heat 4 tablespoons jojoba oil and 1 tablespoon grated beeswax in a stainless steel pot in a saucepan of boiling water. Once melted, remove from heat and quickly whisk in 7 drops lavender oil and ¼ teaspoon vitamin E oil. Then place the bowl into a shallow pan of ice water and continue whisking as you add 1 teaspoon honey. Transfer the balm into your lip balm container and leave for 3 hours.

Treating Eczema

Eczema is a dry skin condition that can cause the skin to become itchy, red and cracked. Applying neat lavender oil to small patches of affected skin can boost the healing process.

Haircare

Detangling Spray

Pour some cool distilled water into a pump-action plastic bottle. Add 1 tablespoon aloe vera, 1 tablespoon glycerine and 8 drops lavender oil. Replace the lid and shake well and spray onto the hair; your comb should now glide through.

Head Lice

Up to one in five school children have those nasty head lice at any one time in the UK and up to 80 per cent of head lice are now resistant to insecticide treatment.

You can use a mixture of 2 drops lavender oil mixed with 1 teaspoon olive oil to remove both the lice and their eggs. Apply to the hair and scalp and leave on overnight – protecting your pillow with a towel. Wash out thoroughly in the morning.

CAUTION: Lavender oil can have a powerful effect if applied to the scalp so always do a patch test. The European Medicines Agency does not recommend using lavender oil on children under 12.

Greasy Hair Scalp Rub

Take 1 tablespoon almond oil and mix with a few drops of lavender essential oil and massage into your scalp.

Dandruff Treatment

You can make your own lavender anti–dandruff shampoo by combining 8 drops each lavender and eucalyptus oils with 1 tablespoon apple cider vinegar. Mix the vinegar/lavender solution with a herbal shampoo containing rosemary and/or thyme.

Shiny Hair Rinse

Sometimes our hair just feels a bit
dull and lifeless. To add shine to
greasy hair, make up an infusion
25 g/1 oz/1 cup dried lavender with
600 ml/1 pint/2½ cups boiled water.
Steep for 15 minutes and strain
through a muslin cloth. Use the liquid
as a final rinse after shampooing.

Treating Alopecia

Alopecia areata is an auto-immune
disease that causes hair loss. One
Scottish study has found that people
who massaged their scalps with
lavender and other essential oils daily
for seven months had more hair
growth than a control group who did
not apply essential oils.

Mix together 3 drops each
lavender and rosemary essential oils,
2 drops each thyme and cedar
wood oils, add 4 teaspoons
grapeseed oil and ½ teaspoon
jojoba oil. Massage the mixture
onto your scalp every night for
five minutes.

Health

Lavender has been used in medicine since ancient times. For over 2,000 years, lavender has been variously used to keep the plague and cholera at bay, as an antiseptic in wound care, to treat insomnia and soothe headaches. In the twenty-first century, lavender is still being used to treat a variety of conditions.

Safe Lavender Use

Pregnancy and Breastfeeding

Lavender oil can have an effect on the central nervous system and should therefore be avoided in pregnancy. However, if used under strict supervision by a qualified midwife and/or aromatherapist, lavender essential oil is thought to be safe to use in labour to induce relaxation and to ease backache and encourage contractions. Use diluted in a carrier oil.

Lavender oil is best avoided whilst breastfeeding.

Sleeping Pills

There is a risk lavender oil could intensify the effects of sedatives such as zolpidem and lorazepam because it induces feelings of sleepiness, so always inform your doctor if you use lavender oil and are on prescription drugs.

CAUTION: Like all herbs, lavender can have powerful effects so use with caution and always consult your doctor if you are taking any prescription medication.

Epilepsy

When lavender or any essential oil is massaged into the skin, tiny molecules pass through the barrier of the skin into tissue and into the bloodstream, travelling to the brain. Inhaled oils also go to the brain via the lungs.

Spike lavender oil has a higher concentration of camphor and is not recommended for use in epilepsy, because it is believed to have a stimulating effect and may trigger seizures. However, lavender oil (except spike lavender) may be useful in preventing seizures if the attacks are triggered by stress as it has a calming effect. This has been backed up by a study by the University of Birmingham, which found that inhaling lavender oil could reduce the number of seizures in epilepsy patients.

A Word of Caution

Because lavender slows down the central nervous system it can intensify the effects of drugs such as tranquillizers and benzodiazepines, so avoid lavender aromatherapy if you are already taking prescription drugs for anxiety.

Hormone Disruption

A study published in the *New England Journal of Medicine* in 2007 found that boys who developed a condition called pre-pubertal gynecomastia (breast development before puberty) had all been using skin preparations containing lavender and tea tree oil .Their symptoms disappeared when use of these products was stopped. The study was only conducted on three boys but the authors concluded lavender products could disrupt the normal male hormones in their bodies. The European Medicines Agency says its use should be avoided in under 12s as there is insufficient safety data.

Others Things to Avoid

Lavender is toxic – do not drink it and do not apply to open wounds. Avoid lavender for two weeks before surgery – it might slow down the central nervous system too much if used in combination with anaesthesia. Lavender may also impair the ability to drive and use machines.

Allergies to Lavender Oil

Some people can be allergic to lavender oil absorbed through the skin. Stop using if you develop nausea, vomiting, headaches, chills or skin irritation.

Internal Health

A Wonder Herb

Scientists have shown that the smell of lavender oil has an effect on the central nervous system and may induce feelings of calm and combat anxiety and depression. It also has antiseptic, astringent and antifungal properties, so is used in natural first-aid products and skin care. Here's our handy reference guide to some of lavender's uses in herbal medicine, antiseptic skin care and aromatherapy.

Headaches

More than 10 million people in the UK get headaches, making them one of the most common everyday health complaints. Lavender is believed to have soothing, calming qualities. However, despite centuries of use there is not a great deal of hard scientific evidence to back up these claims. So does the scientific evidence stack up?

The latest research seems to suggest it does. A study published in 2012 by the University of Tehran tested 47 patients who had been diagnosed with migraine headaches (these are a specific type of severe headache), and divided them into cases and controls. Cases inhaled lavender oil for 15 minutes, and the control group was given liquid paraffin for the same time period. Patients were then asked to record the severity of their headache in 30–minute intervals for two hours. The group who inhaled lavender reported less severe headaches than the control group.

Massage Your Headache Away

Add 1–4 drops lavender oil per tablespoon of carrier oil (almond oil is sweet smelling). Remember – lavender oil is toxic if taken orally. Only use the oil externally or by inhalation. Also, avoid contact with eyes or mucous membranes, such as the lips and nostrils. *See* the safety warnings on pages 75–77.

Make Your Own Headache Balm

Mix together 100 g/3½ oz/¼ cup shea butter, 1 tablespoon grated beeswax, 1 tablespoon grapeseed oil, ¼ teaspoon (or 1 capsule) vitamin E and a blend of 8 drops lavender essential oil, 1 drop jasmine essential oil and 1 drop chamomile or lemon balm. Apply to your temples and the back of your neck to ease headaches.

Emergency DIY Cure

Out and about and feel a headache coming on? Put 3 drops lavender and/or 2 drops peppermint essential oils onto a folded-up tissue. Inhale three long, slow, deep breaths of the aroma. Pause and then take three more deep breaths. Do this up to three times. Keep the oils with you so you can make a pre-emptive strike as soon as you feel your headache starting.

Lavender Brew

Add 2–4 drops lavender oil to 250 ml/8 fl oz/1 cup boiling water and inhale the vapours to ease your headache. If you have asthma or allergies, talk to your doctor before using essential oils. Lavender oil can sometimes cause irritation (see page 76).

Insomnia

Sleep problems are extremely common and affect most of us from time to time, although some people suffer long-term chronic insomnia too. Insomnia is defined as difficulties falling and staying asleep. As any torturer will tell you, sleep deprivation is one of their most effective weapons, leaving the victim disorientated, drowsy and confused. Doctors say the sleep deprived are often some of the most desperate patients they see, with millions of prescriptions written every year for sleeping pills.

Can Lavender Help?

Lavender is a popular folk remedy for sleep problems. It's been used by insomniacs for hundreds of years in muslin bags and sleep pillows, often mixed with other herbs and hops.

But is there any scientific proof? Despite lavender being such a popular remedy, it is under-researched and its popularity is largely based on anecdotal evidence.

The Evidence

The University of Maryland says there *is* evidence that aromatherapy with lavender may slow the activity of the central nervous system, improve sleep quality, promote relaxation and boost mood in people suffering from insomnia.

Lavender Sleep Spray

Try diluting a few drops of lavender oil in some distilled water and decant into a plastic water bottle with a spray action and use it to spray bed linen during ironing. Alternatively, add lavender-scented fabric conditioner to your washing machine (*see* page 34).

Lavender Baths

Add a few drops of lavender essential oil to your bath water and have a relaxing soak before bedtime as part of a winding–down routine. Inhaling the lavender fragrance will help you slow down and relax which may help you drift off to sleep. *See* page 99 for our lavender bath bomb recipe.

Lavender Tea

In Germany, lavender flowers have been approved for treating insomnia, restlessness and nervous stomach conditions. To make lavender tea, you will simply need some fresh lavender and water (*see* page 171 for the recipe). Drink one hour before bedtime.

Make a Lavender Sleep Pillow

These are available to buy in shops but it's simple to make your own with some dried lavender (*see* page 156).

Anxiety Treatment In History

The benefits of lavender for treating anxiety have been acknowledged for centuries. In the seventeenth century, the herbalist Nicholas Culpepper wrote, 'Lavender is of a special good use for all the griefs and pains of the head.' As already mentioned, Florence Nightingale used it to anoint the foreheads of wounded soldiers on her hospital wards to aid relaxation and combat stress.

A Word About Anxiety

Being anxious and feeling worried is very common. About one in 20 people in the UK suffer from Generalized Anxiety Disorder (GAD) – a long-term condition which causes people to feel anxious about a range of situations and issues rather than one specific event.

Anxiety Symptom Spotter

Anxiety becomes a problem if it is inappropriately strong, occurs often and lasts too long, you lose control and have to avoid certain situations.

Anxiety in New Mums

A 2012 research study at the Wellspring Pharmacy in Indianopolis , USA, used

aromatherapy with oil of *Lavandula angustifolia* in women who had just given birth and who were at high risk of anxiety and depression. Twenty-eight were treated with two 15-minute aromatherapy sessions twice a week for four weeks. The research team assessed the women using the Generalized Anxiety Disorder Scale (GAD-7) at the beginning, middle and end of the study, and found significant improvements in anxiety levels at the middle and end points.

Lavender and the Dentist's Waiting Room

If you have a fear of the dentist, you might want to dab a few drops of lavender essential oil on your hankie before your next visit. A 2010 study conducted at King's College London's Dental Institute found patients in a waiting room scented with lavender had lower anxiety levels than those who sat in an unscented room. Although anxiety about future dental visits seems to be unaffected, lavender scent would seem to reduce anxiety among dental patients in the short term.

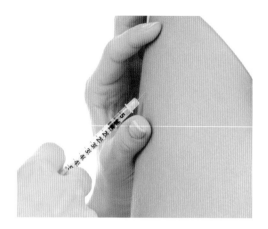

Lavender and Injections

If you hate having injections, a quick whiff of lavender oil might just do the trick and quell some of your anxiety. A study in Korea found that patients who inhaled lavender scent via an oxygen mask had lower stress levels than those who used an ordinary oxygen mask for five minutes. The lavender group also reported less pain when the needle was inserted.

Silexan Capsules For Anxiety

Until recently lavender has been used to treat anxiety via aromatherapy, but a new capsule form of lavender oil is now registered and available in Germany, and may eventually become available in the UK. Silexan is a capsule that contains pharmaceutical–grade lavender oil with

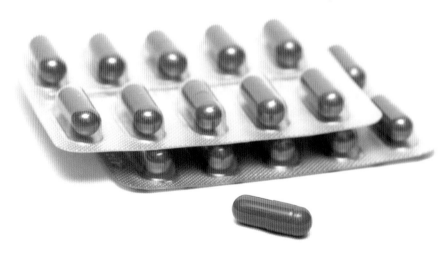

a high ester content (esters are plant compounds and there is a belief that the higher the ester content the more effective the oil). It is distilled from *Lavandula angustifolia* plants.

One study conducted by the University of Vienna published in 2010 treated 221 adults with an anxiety disorder with 80 mg Silexan or a placebo for 10 weeks. Those who took the Silexan had less anxiety and slept better compared to the placebo group. Significant effects were felt after only two weeks of treatment.

Another study which compared the effects of Silexan to Lorazepam – a benzodiazepine drug used to treat anxiety – found after six weeks Silexan was as effective in reducing anxiety symptoms. but without the side effects (including sleepiness). Long–term use of bendodiazepines can also lead to side effects and addiction. so lavender oil may be a better long–term solution.

Why Not Try?

Sprinkle a few drops of lavender on a hanky to help soothe anxiety in stressful situations such as commuting.

CAUTION: Always consult your doctor before coming off any medication.

Mood and Depression

Lavender is widely credited with lifting the spirits and boosting mood, at least in popular folklore. The European Medicines Agency's herbal monograph on *Lavandula angustifolia* says lavender oil is a 'traditional herbal medicine product for the relief of mild stress and exhaustion and a sleep aid', but this is just recognition of its traditional use and not an endorsement of its effectiveness.

So what do the scientists make of these claims? There's actually very little hard scientific evidence that lavender can help with depression. Mostly it's anecdotal reports that have made it so popular.

Influencing Mood

One possible explanation is that if you inhale lavender oil, smell receptors in the nose send chemical messages to a part of the brain known as the limbic region, which influences emotional responses, heart rate and blood pressure.

Antidepressant Effect

Lavandula angustifolia Mill (Lamiacae) is used to treat depression and many herbal medicine textbooks refer to it, but as discussed there is little scientific evidence to support its effectiveness.

However, a study conducted in 2003 at Tehran University investigated using a lavender tincture (60 drops a day at a ratio of 1:5 in 50 per cent alcohol) with the antidepressant imipramine and compared it to using imipramine alone in 40 patients with mild to moderate depression. The combined treatment was more effective than using the antidepressant on its own, the main advantage being that patients got better quicker. (*See* page 104 for our tincture recipe).

Lavender Baths to Boost Mood

Soaking in a lavender bath may perk up your mood, according to research carried out by the University of Wolverhampton. Two groups of women were given either grapeseed oil or lavender oil to use in their bath water for 14 days. Positive mood changes were reported by the group who had added lavender oil to their baths and they also had fewer negative responses about the future.

Stress Relief

These days lavender is listed as an ingredient of any number of stress-busting products on the shelves of chemists and supermarkets. Bath soaks, shower creams and muscle rubs all claim that lavender will help you unwind and recover from the daily stresses and strains of everyday living.

And there certainly is some evidence that lavender oil may affect stress levels. One study published in 2008 showed that inhaling lavender has been shown to reduce salivary markers for stress following a stress-inducing maths exercise – enough to make anyone break out in a sweat!

Lavender in Your Lunch Break

Lavender may be just the boost you need to stop your performance flagging mid-afternoon at work. One Japanese study found that the dip in performance most office workers experience in the afternoon was reduced by exposure to lavender aroma in the afternoon break. The lead researcher explained this effect by arguing that lavender reduced arousal levels during the recess so that concentration levels increased again in the following testing block.

Soothe Agitation

Elderly people with dementia were less agitated when treated with lavender inhalation than a control group, according to research by the Chinese University of Hong Kong. The researchers concluded that lavender aromatherapy might be a useful additional treatment option to us alongside standard treatments.

Spatial Skills

It seems that lavender scent might be able to help improve your spatial skills. So far this work has only been done in rats, but the results look promising. A 2011 study found that rats who inhaled lavender oil for seven continuous days had significantly lower levels of anxiety-type behaviour. Their spatial memory, which enables themselves to find their way around, also improved. The authors of the study say exposure to lavender inhalation could reverse spatial memory problems.

Asthma

Asthma is a long-term condition that can cause a cough, wheezing and breathlessness. It's extremely common, with one in 12 adults and one in 11 children affected. It is a condition that affects the airways – the small tubes that carry air in and out of the lungs. When a person with asthma comes into contact with a trigger, the muscle around the walls of the airways tightens so that the airway becomes narrower. The lining of the airways becomes inflamed and starts to swell. Often sticky mucus or phlegm is produced. All these reactions cause the airways to become narrower and irritated, leading to the symptoms of asthma.

Asthma Relief

Lavender is credited with having anti-inflammatory properties and is sometimes used in aromatherapy combined with peppermint and eucalyptus essential oils to help open airways during a mild asthma attack. However, if you have asthma please discuss all treatment therapies with your doctor.

Bronchitis

Bronchitis is an infection of the main airways of the lungs (bronchi), which causes them to become inflamed and irritated. This causes congestion and breathing problems.

Inhalation of essential lavender oil is believed to help clear the airways and loosen mucus built up in the airways. The aim of treatment is to shift the mucus out of your lungs and airways.

Clearing the Airways

Dissolve a few drops lavender oil in a bowl of hot water and lean over it with a towel over your head for 10–14 minutes. For maximum effectiveness, add a few drops eucalyptus oil. You can also try adding lavender to a hot bath or place a few drops of oil on a terracotta diffuser in the shower and let warm water run over it to release the vapours.

Laryngitis

Laryngitis is the medical name for inflammation and infection of the larynx (vocal chords). Symptoms include a croaky voice, sore throat and pain when you speak. To ease the pain in your throat try massaging it with two drops of lavender oil dissolved in 1 tsp warm sesame oil. Or make an infusion by steeping fresh or dried lavender in hot water, covering and leaving to stand and then inhaling.

CAUTION: Lavender can induce an allergic reaction (see page 76) in some people. Always contact your doctor if you notice any irritation following exposure to lavender oil.

Try a Catarrh Rub

Mix 1 drop each lavender, chamomile, eucalyptus and peppermint essential oils in 2 tablespoons base oil (almond, sesame or olive oil) and use as a chest rub. This will loosen catarrh and help you breathe more easily. You could also add them to a bowl of boiling water and try steam inhalation.

Whooping Cough

Whooping cough is an infection of the lining of the airways. It's known as whooping cough because the main symptom is a hacking cough, which can be followed by a sharp intake of breath that sounds like a 'whoop'. The disease is serious in babies under one (who need to be hospitalized) and young children, but less so in teenagers and adults.

Chest Rub

Lavender oil is not recommended by the European Medicines Agency for children under 12. For teenagers and adults, however, try adding a few drops of lavender oil to a carrier oil with eucalyptus, lavender, chamomile and peppermint, and massaging into the chest and back to ease the cough.

Tonsillitis

Tonsillitis is inflammation of the tonsils, usually due to a viral infection, or sometimes a bacterial infection. It causes a sore throat and coughing, headache and a high temperature. It isn't usually serious and goes away on its own within 3–4 days. If it lasts any longer or you develop breathing difficulties, see a doctor. But any of the remedies above for whooping cough, laryngitis etc. may help ease the symptoms.

Four Thieves Vinegar Recipe

If you're always coming down with bugs try this recipe for Four Thieves Vinegar, a traditional remedy for preventing infections. Folklore has it that four thieves arrested for looting during the Great Plague were released in exchange for this recipe that protected them from the disease.

Blend together 2 teaspoons crushed garlic with 2 teaspoons dried lavender, rosemary, sage and mint and cover with 600 ml/1 pint/2½ cups cider vinegar and leave in a warm place for 14 days in a screw-top jar. Then strain and decant into a clean bottle. Take 2 teaspoons three times a day or add it to a bath.

Aches & Pains

Massage

Aromatherapy massage is a complementary medicine therapy. Using essential lavender oil for muscular aches and strains, as well as easing stress and inducing relaxation is a popular choice, mainly because of its pleasant smell and relaxing qualities. Lavender oil is one of the few essential oils that can be applied neat to the skin. It can also be mixed with a carrier oil such as almond or olive oil.

CAUTION: Do not apply to open wounds.

If you are taking any type of prescription drugs, are pregnant or have epilepsy, always inform your massage practitioner. It may be that it is not safe for you to have an aromatherapy massage. (*See* page 75 for information on lavender and safety).

Lavender Oil in Massage

High quality lavender oil distilled from *Lavandula angustifolia* is used in aromatherapy massage because of its fine fragrance and soothing properties. It also has antiseptic, anti-inflammatory and antibacterial properties.

Massage Your Way to Sleep

A US study published in 2004 looked at the use of massage and aromatherapy in 42 people with advanced cancer. These people were divided into three groups and given either a weekly massage, massages with lavender oil or no massages. Those who had both types of massages slept better and were less depressed than those who had none.

Muscle Aches

Make up your own aromatherapy rub for aching tired muscles, by mixing 2 drops lavender oil (for pain relief), 2 drops of geranium (to tone your muscles) and 1 tablespoon of warm almond oil. To ease tension and spasms, gently massage the affected area with 2 drops of lavender, chamomile, rosemary, thyme or ginger in 1 teaspoon of carrier oil.

You could also try adding a few drops of lavender and some of the above essential oils to hot water and soaking a clean piece of gauze or cloth in it before applying as a hot compress.

Baths

Adding lavender essential oil to your bath water is another way to enjoy its therapeutic effects. A lavender bath is great for soothing aching muscles, boosting healing and easing stress, inducing relaxation and sleep. The European Medicines Agency says traditional use is 1–3 g (about 20–60 drops) essential lavender oil per full bath daily and does not recommend lavender oils for use in children under 12. Add some Epsom salts to soak away muscle aches.

Lavender Bath Bomb

Take some dried lavender flowers and place them in a glass bowl with 1 tablespoon citric acid and 3 tablespoons bicarbonate of soda (baking soda), making sure both the bowl and your hands are dry (any dampness will set the citric acid fizzing!). Add 10 drops lavender oil, 1 teaspoon dried lavender flowers and 1 teaspoon almond oil and mix with a metal spoon. Squeeze into a ball shape and leave for at least 30 minutes to allow the oil to evaporate. Then store in tin foil until ready to use.

Arthritis

There is some evidence that lavender oil massage can help rheumatoid arthritis patients sleep better at night. It is possible that its anti-inflammatory properties soothe inflammation in all types of arthritis.

Pregnancy

These days, lavender oil is not recommended in pregnancy (at least not by the European Medicines Agency), but is sometimes used during labour to soothe backache and strengthen contractions under the supervision of a qualified practitioner.

Research published in 2011 reviewed a trial of women who used aromatherapy during labour (including lavender oil) as an add-on to routine care and pain relief, compared to women who had only standard care. The researchers found no difference between the two groups for pain intensity, assisted vaginal birth, caesarean section or epidural rate. They concluded

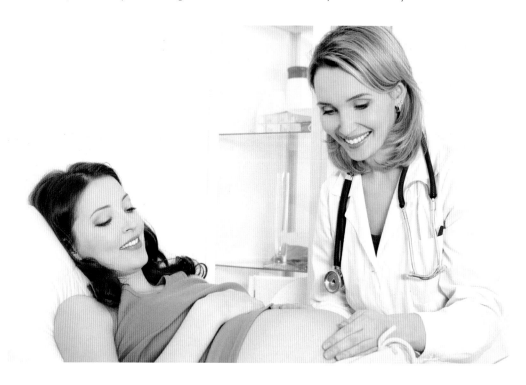

there was insufficient evidence about the benefits of aromatherapy on pain management in labour. However, many women still swear by lavender oil and it's widely available at midwife-led birthing centres.

Period Pain

On a more positive note, modern day research has revealed that massaging the abdomen with a combination of lavender, rose and clary sage essential oils reduced period pain more than massage with a carrier almond oil.

Varicose Veins

Varicose veins are permanently dilated (widened) and twisted veins. Although this can occur in any part of the body, it usually develops in the legs. Symptoms include heavy aching legs. Lavender has astringent toning qualities as well as an anti-inflammatory effect and is thought to improve varicose veins.

Soothing Treatments

To make a compress, combine 3 drops each lavender, chamomile and carrot seed oil with 250 ml/8 fl oz/1 cup cold water, 1 teaspoon calendula and stir. Then soak a muslin cloth in the solution, wring and place over the veins to ease itching and promote healing.

 For soothing gel, mix vegetable gelatine (three sachets), 5 drops lavender essential oil, 150 ml/¼ pint/²⁄₃ cup water and 150 ml/¼ pint/²⁄₃ cup horse chestnut tincture (made by blending 20 conkers with 150 ml/¼ pint/²⁄₃ cup vodka!). Place in a sterilized bottle in a cool dark place for 10–30 days. It keeps in the fridge for three months.

CAUTION: Always do a 24-hour patch test before using, as horse chestnut can cause irritation.

Earache

Earache is one of the worst pains to cope with. Always consult your doctor if you suspect a middle ear infection or a perforated eardrum (symptoms of a perforated eardrum include fluid discharge, hearing loss, tinnitus and pain), as eardrops are not suitable if the eardrum is perforated. If your eardrum isn't perforated, you could make up your own eardrops to ease the pain by mixing 1 teaspoon of warm sesame oil with 2 drops lavender oil, placing 2–3 drops in the ears.

Tinnitus

Tinnitus is a sensation of hearing a persistent noise coming from within the body rather than from outside. This noise is typically a high-pitched ringing, whirring, whining or buzzing, although in some cases sufferers can hear voices or even music. Massaging the neck with 1 teaspoon warm sesame oil mixed with 2 drops lavender oil may bring some relief.

Skin

Cuts and Grazes

For minor cuts and wounds, bathe regularly with a diluted lavender tincture in warm water. To make the tincture, cover chopped lavender flowers with an 80 per cent proof type of alcohol (vodka is good because it is flavourless). Seal and store in a cool dark place for 8 days to a month. Sieve through a muslin cloth and store in a small jar. It keeps for up to five years.

You can also make lavender cream. Customize an unperfumed antiseptic cream with 20 drops of lavender essential oil and apply to cuts to boost healing.

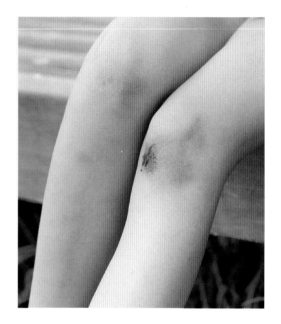

Burns and Scalds

Lavender oils can be applied neat to the skin to minor burns and scalds. Before applying, immerse the area in cold water for 5–10 minutes to cool the skin down. Then repeatedly apply neat lavender oil until the pain starts to subside.

CAUTION: Do not apply to open wounds.

Scars

Lavender oil has painkilling and anti–inflammatory properties which are thought to improve the skin's healing after injury. Specific compounds are believed to reduce redness and swelling. Try applying 2–3 drops of lavender oil diluted with 3 drops of camomile oil after an injury to prevent excessive scarring.

Another combination to try is applying equal parts lavender oil and aloe vera gel to the injury and covering with a sterile dressing. Massaging the area with a night cream to which you've added 2–3 drops of lavender oil may also boost healing.

CAUTION: Do not apply to broken skin. Always seek medical advice if the area is large and/or infected.

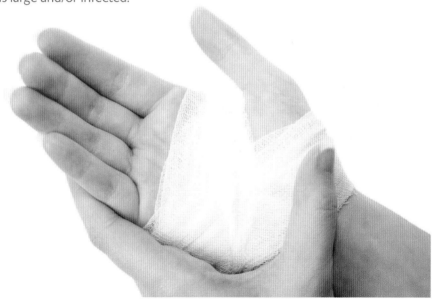

Make a Lavender Skin Soother

The following recipe may ease skin inflammation and minor burns. Take $^2/_3$ cup fresh lavender flowers and cover with 600 ml/1 pint/$2^1/_2$ cups freshly boiled water and leave to cool.

Scabies

These parasites cause intense itching by laying eggs under the skin. Soothe the itching by mixing a tea of antimicrobial herbs including lavender, thyme and peppermint and adding them to a hot bath every night. You can also add 2 drops of lavender oil to a carrier oil and apply to the skin, after you have dried off.

Treating Wasp Stings

Remove the sting with the blunt edge of a butter knife/edge of a credit card and apply vinegar to neutralize the alkaline venom. Apply as often as needed until the pain and swelling have subsided. To prevent infection, add 1 drop of lavender or tea tree oil to each tablespoonful of vinegar.

Bee Stings

Remove the sting with
tweezers, taking care not
to burst the venom sac.
Bee venom is acidic so to
neutralize it, apply an
alkaline solution of
bicarbonate of soda
(baking soda) (1
teaspoonful in about 1
tablespoonful water),
adding 1 drop of lavender
to the solution.

Insect Bites

When an insect bites, it releases saliva that can cause skin around the bite to become red,
swollen and itchy. Treat the bite by washing the affected area and placing a cold compress
(a flannel or cloth soaked in cold water) to reduce swelling. You can also apply neat lavender
oil to reduce inflammation or itching.

Protection Against Insects

Spike lavender oil has a higher camphor content, which is repellent to insects, so is
often used to make commercial insect repellents and mothballs. Try applying a 3 per cent
dilution of essential lavender oil to exposed parts of the skin or use 1–2 per cent dilution
for facial skin.

Psoriasis

Psoriasis is an auto–immune disorder which causes dry patches of skin, causing itching and pain. Your doctor can prescribe medication for this condition, including steroid creams and moisturizers, but you may find mixing lavender and evening primrose oil together and applying to skin patches eases the inflammation.

CAUTION: Do not apply to open wounds or broken skin.

Impetigo

Impetigo is a bacterial infection of the skin that usually starts off as a red rash or fluid–filled blisters that scab over. Antibiotics from your doctor may be needed, but you can soothe the area by cleaning it with cotton wool soaked in lavender water or an infusion.

Cool Down Sunburn

We've all done it – spent too long in the sunshine and been burnt. If your skin looks pink or even red and feels

hot – cool down in a cool bath and add 5 drops each of lavender and chamomile oils and throw in 200 g/ 7 oz/scant 1 cup bicarbonate of soda (baking soda) to draw out the heat. Another variation is to add 8 tablespoons cider vinegar and 8 drops lavender oil. Seek medical attention if your symptoms are severe and you feel unwell.

Use a Spray

Mix up 1 teaspoon witch hazel with 150 ml/¼ pint/ ⅔ cup aloe vera juice, 50 ml/2 fl oz/¼ cup rose water and 10 drops lavender oil for a soothing spray that can be applied to sore skin.

Try a Compress

Make up the lavender tea recipe on page 171 and soak a piece of gauze in it. Then apply directly to the skin to soothe any itching or burning.

Hands and Feet

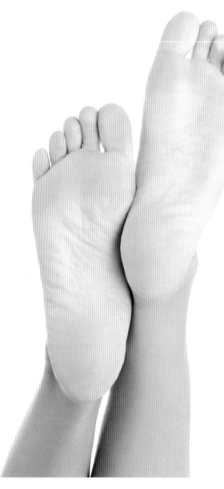

Athlete's Foot

Even at low concentrations, lavender has been shown to have highly potent anti-fungal properties. Lavender oil contains a compound called alpha-pinene, also found in rosemary and turpentine. This could be increasingly important, as there have been reports of increasing resistance to anti-fungal drugs.

Athlete's foot is a fungal skin infection that causes dry, scaly skin patches to form on the soles of the feet. Try soaking your feet twice a day in a strong lavender tea solution (*see* the recipe on page 171). Add other anti-fungal oils such as tea tree oil.

Smelly Feet

Foot odour can be highly embarrassing and anti-social. Try washing your feet, thoroughly drying them and then applying neat lavender oil to kill bacteria. Do this every night before bedtime. You could also put some scented lavender bags in your shoes overnight.

Nail Infections

Fungal nail infections affect about 3 per cent of the population. They more commonly affect the toenails than the fingernails. Although anti-fungal medication is effective, some people do suffer side effects, including headaches, itching, nausea, upset stomach and loss of taste.

As lavender essential oil has anti-fungal properties it makes a good natural treatment for fungal nail infections. Try washing your feet thoroughly, clipping away as much of the affected nail as possible, drying and applying 1 drop of neat lavender oil directly into the nail bed, every morning and evening. Trim the toenail weekly and gradually the lavender oil will destroy the fungus.

Brittle Nails

Lavender oil is also believed to help speed up cracked or damaged surfaces of the nail and is often used in manicures and pedicures. It also soothes the inflammation of severely dry cuticles as well as helping to heal dry skin.

Home & Garden

Outdoors

Lavender is fairly easy to grow because it is drought tolerant; in fact in some countries of the Mediterranean it grows wild and is regarded as a weed. In parts of Australia it is so invasive that it is regarded as a pest. But mostly lavender is widely grown because it attracts bees, needed to pollinate flowers. Conversely it also repels other insects, so can be used to repel pests.

Pests and Insects

Attracting Bees

Lavender is well known as a plant that will attract bees into a garden. Research carried out by Queen Mary's College at the University of London has found that bee colonies that favour purple flowers were more successful because the flowers produced the most nectar. The researchers found that inexperienced bees had a strong preference for the colour purple, partly explaining why lavender plants are such a magnet.

Why We Need Bees

Bees are important pollinators for a wide range of flowers, garden vegetables and commercial crops, but sadly their numbers are declining. Planting lavender not only gives bees a rich source of nectar, but its mid–summer flowering also fills an important 'gap' when bees' other food sources can be tricky to find.

Plant Protector

The added bonus with lavender is that it repels other insects such as mosquitoes, fleas and moths (hence its popularity in mothballs and insect repellents). This is due to the fact that the plant has amongst others camphor and eucalyptus oils, which insects generally hate. Planting lavender amongst your other plants can help protect them from certain unwanted pests.

Bug Buster

Lavender oil has insect–repelling properties. French/Spanish lavender has a higher camphor content and is widely grown to make insect repellent and mothballs. Growing lavender on your terrace could stop annoying mosquitoes and other flying bugs bothering you on summer evenings. Cotton lavender has the strongest insect–repellent properties. It's not strictly a lavender, however, but a member of the Asteraceae family (aster, daisy or sunflower).

DIY Insect Sprays

If you're sitting outside on a summer evening and being nibbled by mosquitoes and the like, try this home remedy for repelling the little blighters. Fill a bottle with cut lavender flowers and cover with white vinegar, seal and set aside to infuse for 2 weeks, remembering to shake it every day. Strain the lavender from the liquid using a muslin cloth and then return to the plastic bottle. Spray your skin whenever you are outside, taking care to cover up with clothing as much as possible in the evenings.

Vehicles

Lavender Deodorizer

Banish cigarette smells or other unpleasant odours in your car by making up your own lavender deodorizing spray and spritz the upholstery with five or six squirts. To make the spray, mix some distilled water with 120 ml/4 fl oz/$\frac{1}{2}$ cup vodka and add 8 drops of lavender oil and shake. Add 2 drops of bergamot oil, 4 drops of clove oil and 2 drops of peppermint, shaking the mixture between each addition.

Car Disinfectant

You can also try combining lavender water in equal parts with white vinegar to make a natural antiseptic spray. Combine 1 litre/2 pints/4 cups distilled water with 5 tablespoons vodka in a glass or ceramic bowl, add 30 drops lavender essential oil and then decant into a bottle. Leave 24 hours in the fridge before using. If you add it in equal parts to white vinegar it makes a good all-purpose disinfectant.

CAUTION: Avoid direct contact with the skin when making up the mixture.

Pet Care

Lavender is a useful ingredient for various pet care products. It's used to repel fleas, banish 'doggy' and/or cat pee odours in the home and can calm over-anxious dogs. As with its use in humans, be aware that lavender can have quite a powerful effect, so use with caution at first to see if your pet has an allergic reaction. Lavender oil should never be given orally to pets and, if applied to the skin, needs to be diluted and patch tested in minute quantities for 24 hours first. Its use should also be avoided in cats.

Cleaning

Caution with Lavender

Only *Lavandula angustifolia* oil should be used. Lavender hybrid (lavandin) oils are harsher and may have a more powerful effect in animals. Lavender (and most other essential oils) should not be used around cats. Lavender essential oil should not be taken internally as it may cause liver or kidney damage. Lavender essential oil should not be used on pregnant or nursing dogs.

A Handy Herb

With a bottle of lavender essential oil in your store cupboard, you'll be well equipped to tackle clearing up after your pet, from keeping their bedding clean and fragrant to ridding your pets – and your home – of fleas. A small amount of lavender oil added to water and other cleaning and washing items can banish animal odours and leave your home and pet smelling sweet.

Deodorize and Disinfect

Use the recipe for lavender disinfectant on page 40 for a non-toxic clean up which will freshen up floors and work surfaces. You can also dilute lavender oil in distilled water and use it to spray dog bedding and blankets – 1 teaspoon lavender oil for every 500 ml/18 fl oz/2 cups water should be safe, but always check for signs of sensitivity in your pet before cleaning a large area and make sure the room is well ventilated.

Flea Repellent

Lavender repels fleas, although it doesn't kill them. If you don't want to use harsh chemicals on your dog try spraying them with a lavender water mixture. Take fresh lavender flowers and soak them overnight in a sealed container with distilled water. Drain out the flowers with a sieve the next day and transfer the remaining liquid into a clean pump–action bottle and spray your pet's coat.

CAUTION: Always patch test any sprays for 24 hours to check for sensitivity. Do not use on cats.

Animal Behaviour

Lavender For Car Sickness

If your dog gets travel sick in the car, try this handy tip. Soak a cotton wool ball in lavender essential oil and leave in the car for 30 minutes before your departure. Remove before you start your journey. The aroma should help with your dog's nausea and help him stay calm.

CAUTION: Always make sure the lavender oil you are using is of therapeutic grade and does not contain any contaminants.

Burning lavender oil

If you're burning diluted lavender in a diffuser at home, don't unintentionally overdose your pets. Vets say that if you overuse lavender oil it can lead to the development of allergic responses. It's worth talking to your vet for advice.

Lavender For Calming Dogs

Some dogs can be hyperactive or anxious. Lavender essential oil has calming properties. Make up a lavender spray with 250 ml/8 fl oz/1 cup water and 10 drops pure lavender essential oil. Try spraying your dog's coat before leaving him alone or before a stressful trip to the vets.

CAUTION: Animals have a sensitive sense of smell. If an animal does not like a particular odour, do not enforce its use.

Growing Lavender

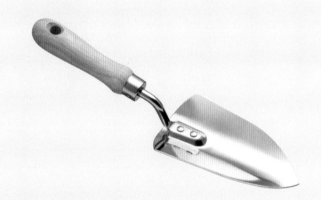

Getting Started

Part of lavender's universal appeal to gardeners all over the world is that it is an unfussy, drought-tolerant plant. Ideally it likes a sunny spot and well-drained soil, but it can tolerate a wide range of weather conditions. Some types are frost-hardy and will grow anywhere from the Mediterranean to Northern Europe, the US and Australia. It earns its place in the garden because it ticks so many boxes – long flowering season, pretty flowers, delicious fragrance and a magnet for bees – vital to flower pollination.

The Joys of Lavender

The Old Favourite

Because lavender is so easy to grow, it's literally grown everywhere. You will spot it in tiny pots and window boxes on the balconies and windowsills of city flats, compact urban gardens and rambling cottage gardens alike. You'll also see lavender growing in public parks, in the middle of roundabouts and growing wild at the side of the road, but it's equally at home in the gardens of stately homes.

Choose How to Grow It

Although lavender is one of the easiest plants to grow, there are still some pit-falls, namely problems posed by water-logged soil, the rosemary beetle and the folly of failing to cut flowers back every year.

Tools & Equipment

Trowel

You won't need much in terms of gardening equipment to plant and care for a lavender bush, but one thing you'll need is a trowel. This is a tool with a pointed, scoop-shaped metal blade and a handle. It is used for breaking up earth, digging small holes, especially for planting, weeding and mixing in fertilizer or other additives, and transferring plants to pots. The best-quality trowels have wooden handles and metal blades.

Secateurs

Another handy piece of equipment is secateurs. You'll need these to cut back the lavender bush once a year. Secateurs have short handles and you can operate them with one hand. A spring between the handles causes the jaws to open again after closing. When not in use, the jaws may be held closed by a safety catch or by a loop holding the handles together.

Watering Can

Lavender plants are fairly low maintenance and only need watering during certain periods, however when they do, a watering can is ideal. Buy one with a detachable rose.

Where to Grow

Containers or Soil?

Most types of lavender can be grown in the ground, but if you have clay soil which is prone to water logging or perhaps you want to grow on a balcony, you may prefer to grow them in a pot with some grit/gravel instead. Equally, if you choose a type of lavender that isn't frost–hardy, you will have to plant it in a pot so you can move it indoors.

Planting in a Pot

Choose a large pot with a diameter of between 30–40 cm, and a deep one which will allow for root growth. Use a gritty, free-draining compost. Gardening experts recommend adding up to 25 per cent by volume of coarse grit to a loam–based compost. Keep the compost moist, but never overwater as lavender hates water–logged soil. Use a balanced fertilizer to encourage growth.

Terracotta Pots

Terracotta pots are readily available in garden centres and are very popular. You can buy them in many different shapes and sizes to fit into your space. They are a good choice for growing lavender because they wick away moisture from the plants, which means the risk of overwatering is reduced. The material is durable and attractive; they are quite heavy which makes them ideal for exposed areas; and there is no risk of them blowing over in the wind, even with tall plants in them.

Terracotta in Depth

Terracotta pots are sturdy and, if looked after, can last many years. Unglazed pots are available in the traditional terracotta colour but you can buy glazed ones in all colours. Terracotta is easily recycled after use and is safe for growing food crops. However, they also have some disadvantages. Terracotta pots break easily if dropped or knocked. Some cheaper pots crack in the frost because water gets into the material, freezes and expands; they can also be too porous. Glazed pots can stop this happening, but can be expensive.

Plastic Pots

Plastic pots are readily available, lightweight, cheap and a popular choice, but they're not suitable for growing lavender as they retain water. Even though they are better for gardeners who occasionally forget to water, they can keep soil too wet which leads to rotting roots.

PVC Containers

Many window boxes are now made from PVC, which makes them very stable. Due to their popularity, prices are coming down all the time, making PVC one of the cheaper options. The many advantages of PVC containers include the fact that they are rot and moisture free, unattractive to insects, do not crack or warp, can be painted to look like wood, and are also a cheaper choice. However, PVC is made from non-renewable resources and is difficult to recycle, so it's not the ideal material for end disposal.

Raised Beds

Raised beds are ideal if you have a decent-sized patio to build them on, and are a good choice for lavender as you can control the environment of the plot and ensure it doesn't become water-logged. You can buy pre-made beds that you slot together, or you can make your own from a variety of materials. Raised-bed gardening is very popular, even for people who have large gardens, as there are several advantages to them over an open plot, such as easier weeding.

Raised beds are usually made of wood and are basically large boxes of compost. They are usually 1–1.2 m (3–4 ft) wide and any length to suit the size of your plot. You can make them anything from 30 cm (12 in) deep to waist high, which is perfect for people who find it hard to bend or kneel.

Raising the Base

All containers need to be kept slightly above ground level to let air flow underneath and to prevent the plant and pot sitting in water. This is especially important for wooden containers that will rot if left in contact with water. Some stone troughs have built-in 'legs' to achieve this. For other containers you'll need to buy or make your own. Old bricks or chunks of wood are ideal. Alternatively you can buy terracotta 'legs' which sit under the corners of your chosen container.

Drainage Holes

Whatever type of container you've chosen, it will need drainage holes at the bottom. Most plants will die if their roots are kept in water for too long. The majority of containers already have holes in them, but you will have to make them yourself if yours doesn't.

Drainage Material

You will need a 5 cm (2 in) layer of suitable drainage material. Traditionally this would be stones or gravel or broken crockery.

Preparing to Plant

Lavender-Friendly Soil

Lavender grows best in moderately fertile alkaline soils in full sun. Think of the lavender fields of Provence in France to get some idea of perfect growing conditions. Having said that however, lavender can also be grown on acid and neutral soils and even in heavy clay (with some extra help), so it's very adaptable.

More Soil Tips

Gardening experts warn that lavender won't do as well or last as long on heavy clay soils (it may become too woody at the base for instance), because it will be prone to water logging

and the roots may rot – particularly in winter. You can get over this by surrounding the base of the plant with gravel to improve drainage and adding some organic matter in spring. plus some lime to neutralize the acidity of the soil. Growing lavender in raised beds will also help keep the roots drier.

Fertilizers For Lavender

Lavender doesn't generally need a lot of feeding. although if grown in a pot some slow–release fertilizer capsules may be beneficial. Avoid using nitrogen–based fertilizers because these will encourage weak, sappy growth. Instead add some potash around the base of the plant in spring and this will encourage more prolific flowering.

Where To Position

Lavender plants thrive in full sun. although they will also tolerate partial shade. Choose a sunny spot, such as at the base of a sunny wall. The popular English Hidcote lavender (*see* page 134) likes a sheltered east–. south– or west-facing aspect, ideally sheltered from the wind.

Garden Planning

You can plant lavender alongside walls and pathways so they give off fragrance when you brush past them. They are versatile enough to look good in gravel gardens, flower borders, pots and cottage gardens (with roses), as well as coastal and drought-resistant gardens. Lavender also makes attractive ground cover for banks and slopes. Plant under a south-facing window for fragrance or alongside a patio so the scent wafts into the house.

Lavandula angustifolia (Hidcote) English lavender is an ideal lavender for hedges and should be planted 30 cm (12 in) apart.

Growing From Seed

For hardy lavenders, sow seed in spring in potted compost under cover at 18°C/65°F either in a greenhouse or indoors. If you already have lavender bushes, you can collect the black seed from the flower heads in summer. Be warned – it can take up to three months for the seed to germinate, so patience is required!

Propagating Lavender

Lavender grows easily from cuttings – the trick is to select from this season's growth in late summer. Choose a stem that hasn't flowered and is free of pests and disease. Pull away from the main stem with a thin strip of bark, or heel, still attached. Then strip the stem of any leaves lower down and insert the bare stem into compost in a 10 cm (3 in) pot. You can also dip the cut end of each cutting into rooting hormone.

Use the same pot for several cuttings. Then water and cover with a polythene bag in a warm place in the shade. Within a few weeks, roots should have been established and you'll see new growth. Protect cutting under glass in winter.

Planting in the Ground

Late spring is the best time to plant lavender; the soil temperature should be 18–24°C/65–75°F. Always check the instructions for the type of lavender you are planting and note its spread and height so that you leave enough space. Dig some grit into the flowerbed and add an extra couple of handfuls of grit under each plant so they are slightly raised up – this will ensure they never get water–logged.

Planting Tips

Pinch out the tops of any leaves and stalks that are taller than the rest of the plant. This will encourage the plant to become bushier. Also cut off all the flower stems after planting – this will encourage the plant to lay down a good root system and develop foliage. If your soil is too heavy and not well drained, dig a large hole and mix in sand and gravel to the soil that will surround the lavender plant.

Spacing Your Plants

Lavender can make a beautiful companion plant to other plants in your garden, and create some lovely colour dynamics. If you want to plant your lavenders randomly with other

plants, depending on the ultimate size of your lavender. leave 45–90 cm (18–36 in) between plants. If you have space, try to plant in groups of threes or fives, as this will give you an effective drift of colour.

Planting a Lavender Hedge

To create a hedge, expert lavender growers recommend planting lavender plants 30–40 cm (12–16 in) apart for a lavender that will grow up to 60 cm (2 ft) wide. For a wider lavender over 60 cm (2 ft), leave 40–50 cm (16–20 in) between plants.

Creating a Herb Garden

Lavender can be grown as part of a herb garden alongside rosemary, thyme, lemon balm, parsley and sage either in a raised bed or garden border. Herbs are not only useful for cooking and household remedies, but are also wonderfully aromatic and fill your garden or terrace with heady fragrance.

Maintenance

Now that you've chosen to grow that beautiful and aromatic lavender in your garden or home, you need to know how to take care of it. Luckily lavender is fairly low maintenance, only needing a little watering and care, although there are some nasty pests and diseases to watch out for – prevention is often better than cure!

Plant Care

Watering Lavender

Lavender is a drought–tolerant plant and needs very little watering once it is established. If you are growing lavender in a pot, ensure it has adequate drainage as water–logged roots will rot and the plant will die.

Some gardening experts say it is better to give pot lavender one really good water and then wait for it to dry out, rather than watering little and often. As discussed on pages 127 and 136, adding grit and gravel will help prevent water logging.

Young Lavender Plants

Young plants that are not yet established do need more watering than adult plants, but they still don't need as much

water as other types of plants. Feel the soil in the container and check it hasn't dried out and top up regularly.

What To Do in a Downpour

If you're having a spell of torrential rain and worried your lavender will become water-logged, you could try covering it with a large box or crate. If you are growing your lavender in containers, try moving them indoors or into a garage for protection.

Pruning Lavender

If you don't prune your lavender regularly it can become woody and leggy, and shorten the life of the plant. Hard pruning after flowering every year can prolong the life of the plant and ensure it stays bushy and compact if done regularly and at the right time.

The optimum time to prune is late summer, when flowering is over. This allows enough time for the plant to recover and push out new shoots before winter. Some experts say that French lavender should be cut back in the spring after its first flowering. There's no point just snipping off this year's flowers either – the pruning will have to be far harsher than that if you are going to stop the plant going all woody next year. Be cruel to be kind.

On established plants use secateurs to remove flower stalks and about 2.5cm (1in) of the current year's growth, making sure that some green growth remains (do not cut into old wood).

Garden Pests

Grey Mould

Grey mould *(Botrytis cinerea)* is a common airborne fungus that attacks lavender, causing a fuzzy grey mould on affected areas. Remove dead leaves and dispose of them and avoid overcrowded, humid growing conditions.

Sage Leaf Hopper

The adult sage leaf hopper *(Eupteryx melissae)* is 3 mm ($^1/_{10}$ in) long, with a white body tinged with green and brown, and black spots on its wings. It feeds on lavender, mint, oregano, rosemary, sage, basil, thyme and lemon balm and lays its eggs on the underside of leaves. Damage shows up as white or yellow spots. The best way to limit damage is to isolate plants that have become infected, removing dead leaves and burning them.

Cuckoo Spit

This appears as white 'froth' on the stems and leaves of lavender plants in the spring and summer. It also affects rosemary, roses, dahlias and fuchsias. The yellow–green froghoppers inside the bubbles are around 6 mm ($^1/_5$ in) long and suck the plant sap. The only time they are likely to cause damage is if they attack young plant shoots. The best way to deal with it is to rinse the bubbles off with water.

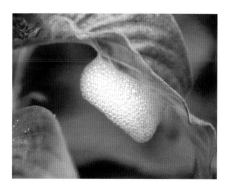

Rosemary Beetle

The rosemary beetle (*Chrysolina americana*) eats the leaves of lavender plants and others including rosemary, sage and thyme. It is a distinctive metallic green with purple stripes on its wings and measures about 8 mm ($\frac{1}{3}$ in). If a lavender plant is being attacked, the foliage will be discoloured and it will have dried edges where the beetle and grubs have been feeding.

Tackling the Problem

You can kill the beetles with insecticides such as pyrethrum, but this should not be used during the flowering season as it can also kill bees. Wait until autumn to spray. A more environmentally friendly way of tackling rosemary beetles is to place a newspaper underneath the plant and shake the stems to dislodge the beetles.

Companion Planting

Good Companions

Lavender is not only pretty and fragrant, but can also have benefits when it is planted as a companion or guardian to other plants. Its added value to the garden is that it attracts bees because it is a rich source of nectar, but conversely it also repels other pests, including mice, rabbits, moths and ticks. It also provides a silvery/grey backdrop for other flowers in your borders, contrasting especially with those in bright colours. The following are some suggestions for companion plants for lavender.

Roses and Lavender

Lavender makes a stunning backdrop for roses and also attracts bees and butterflies. The combination of scents from the two plants in flower in summer creates a heady aroma. A low-growing lavender provides decorative ground cover for a tall, leggy rose bush, and the lavender flowers also provide interest in the border between the summer blooms of roses. Lavender looks particularly good with deep red roses.

Echinacea Cone Flowers

Echinacea (cone flowers) look like giant long-stemmed daisies and come in a variety of colours including pink, yellow, bright orange and white. They can reach heights of up to 1 m (3¼ ft) and enjoy the same sunny conditions as lavender. They bloom in late summer and their height and colour makes a vivid contrast to a backdrop of silvery/grey lavender. Remember to plant lavender at least a foot away from roses so as not to interfere with their root system.

Rosemary

Rosemary is a perennial herb that enjoys the same dry, sunny conditions as lavender. Like lavender, it has a beautiful fragrance and is a perfect companion to lavender in the kitchen garden. Rosemary blooms with small pink or white flowers in late spring, just before lavender begins to bloom. Rosemary can reach heights up to 1.5 m (5 ft) and the dark green foliage looks stunning beside the purple spike flowers of lavender.

Other Silver Plants

Other ideas for planting include combining lavender with other plants with silver foliage – these look particularly stunning at night. Try *Stachys byzantina* 'silver carpet' as a complementary border filler that will shimmer at night. Another option is wild garlic, which produces white flowers but be prepared for a garlic odour. Helichrysum, otherwise known as the curry plant, produces yellow flowers at the same time as lavender in late summer. Artichoke 'green globe' and various artemisias such as Southernwood (*Artemisia abrotanum*) with its yellow flowers and feathery green foliage are also great companions to lavender.

A Dash of White

Offset the silver with white-flowering plants including 'iceberg' roses, agapanthus, feverfew and daisies.

Vegetable Patches

Lavender is repellent to rabbits, mice and moths, all of which can wreak havoc on a vegetable patch or allotment. Plant lavender around a cabbage patch, veg garden or allotment to protect your home-grown food.

Harvesting Lavender

The Right Time To Pick

Hardy English lavenders and bract lavenders should be harvested in summer, just as they open and before they are in full bloom. Try to catch them when the flowers are only one third open, as the flowers keep a stronger colour when cut at this stage.

As a rough guide, cut around one third to one half off the top of your plant each year, but don't cut into 'old' wood. Make sure you harvest a month before you anticipate the first frost, so the plant has time to harden off.

How to Cut

Cut your flowers on a dry and sunny day. If the day is humid or misty, delay harvesting as lavender could become prone to mildew. Wait until the dew has dried off the plants and harvest before the hottest part of the day or the oil will dry out.

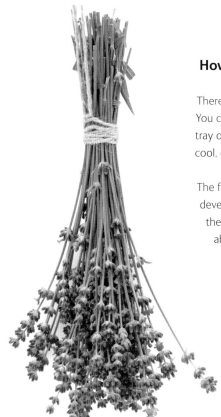

How to Dry

There are several methods for drying lavender. You can either dry the stems loose on a flat tray or hang them up in bunches to dry in a cool, dark place.

The following method helps avoid mildew developing. Tie each flower separately, close to the cut end with a long piece of string. Leave about 2 cm (¾ in) between each stem to allow air to circulate between the stems whilst hanging up for drying and avoid them going mouldy. Knot the ends of your string together to form a loop and hang the 'chain' of stems up in a cool, dark place for four weeks.

Handy Hint

Use elastic bands for lavender bunches. Some lavender growers swear by rubber bands because they say lavender stems shrink when they are drying and the rubber contracts too. If the bunches are tied with raffia, the lavender will end up slipping out and falling on the floor.

Lavender Oil

There are basically three types of lavender oil. True lavender oil is made from *Lavandula angustifolia*. It has a higher plant ester content, which means it is gentler. It is useful in easing muscle pain, headaches, insomnia and burns.

Spike lavender essential oil has a stronger, more stimulating effect on the body, so should not be used for insomnia, anxiety or burns, or in people with epilepsy. You need less of it to get the effects and experts have said it should be used with caution.

Lavandin oil is made from the plant *Lavandula × intermedia* (*see* page 19). It has a higher camphor content with a strong medicinal scent, rather than the sweeter floral smell of true lavender. The plants have a higher yield of oil and it's cheaper than true lavender oil and widely used in soaps and perfumed products.

Distillation of Lavender Oil

Lavender oil is produced via a process called steam distillation. This is a method of separating mixtures based on differences in volatilities of components in a boiling liquid mixture. It is a physical separation process rather than a chemical reaction.

Commercial Distillation

Lavender is packed in a mesh basket and lowered into a stainless steel still (apparatus used for making alcohol), then the lid is put on and bolted down. Steam is then introduced under pressure into the bottom of the still. The steam at 100°C/212°F rapidly rises through the lavender, heating it up.

When heated by the steam the lavender oil boils, expands, bursts out of the oil sac in the flowers and rises in vapour form with the steam. The steam and oil vapour pass through a pipe into a water–cooled condenser. Here both are cooled back to water and minute lavender oil droplets. The lavender oil separates and floats on the top of the water.

Crafts

Around the Home

Dried lavender is highly scented and can be used in a variety of home craft projects from potpourri and hand-sewn sleep pillows to table decorations and scented stationery. You can use your own home-grown lavender or buy dried lavender from farm shops and specialist outlets. Home-made gifts are often inexpensive to make but can create a lasting impression on the recipients because of the time, thought and effort they require. It really is the thought that counts. The project doesn't have to be elaborate either – some simple stitching on crisp white muslin takes only minutes but has a big impact.

History of Potpourri

Potpourri is the name given to mixtures of aromatic dried flower petals and herbs used as room scent and to add fragrance to wardrobes and drawers. French in origin, it means 'rotten flowers'. Potpourris originated in seventeenth-century France where layers of dried herbs and flowers were covered with sea salt and left to ferment. Eventually spices were added to fix a scent and then they would be stored in pots for use as a home fragrance and to protect clothing from moths during storage.

Ingredients Used in Potpourris

Lavender was – and still is – a popular ingredient in potpourri because it is sweet smelling, has sleep–inducing qualities and can also repel insects. Other common ingredients include dried rose petals, lemon peel, orange peel, lemon balm, rosemary, cloves, cinnamon bark, cypress wood and marjoram. The mixture's fragrance is traditionally set with a spice. It's used in bowls around the home or sewn into sachets for use in wardrobes and drawers.

Traditional Potpourris

Mix 1 part dried lavender flowers with 4 parts dried rose buds and petals, chamomile flowers and/or other dried fragrant garden herbs. Add a few drops of lavender essential oil and store in a sealed plastic container with a pinch of orris root powder or ground spice to fix the scent.

Spicy Lavender Potpourri

This is a good recipe to help keep both musty smells and moths at bay. Press 200 g/7 oz/10 cups lavender leaves together, cover with rock salt in a large jar and add 75 g/3 oz/1 cup coriander seeds and 125 g/4 oz/1 cup mixed, crushed cinnamon and nutmeg, with ½ teaspoon lavender oil. Weigh it down with a large object and leave for 10 days and then break up the mixture and leave for another 10 days. Divide into sachets or other storage containers suitable for wardrobes and cupboards.

Lavender Muslin Sachets

This pouch doesn't even need any sewing. Draw a circle on a 15 cm (5 in) square of thin muslin cloth and cut out the circle. Remove the dried flower buds from 10 sprigs of lavender and put them in the middle of the circle, then bring the edges together to form a pouch. Then tie with a 15 cm (5 in) length of ribbon.

Make a Victorian Sleep Pillow

Lavender can induce sleepiness and sleep pillows containing dried lavender have been used for centuries for this purpose. It's simple to make a muslin pillow by cutting out two pieces of fabric each 35 x 30 cm (14 x 12 in) and stitching round three sides, then filling with dried flowers.

Mix 450 ml/³⁄₄ pint/1³⁄₄ cups dark red or pink scented rose petals with 300 ml/¹⁄₂ pint/1¹⁄₄ cups lavender flowers in a bowl and add 150 ml/¹⁄₄ pint/²⁄₃ cup rosemary leaves and 300 ml/ ¹⁄₂ pint/1¹⁄₄ cups elder flowers. Add 3 teaspoons lavender and orris mixture (make this up a couple of days previously using 125 g/4 oz orris root to 1 tablespoon essential oil).

Sew four lace handkerchiefs together in a square and then cut 45 cm (1¹⁄₂ ft) plain white cotton backing to the same size and then turn in the edges by the depth of the lace so the square fits the fabric area of the four handkerchiefs. Use a sewing machine to stitch three sides of the fabric, leaving one side open so you can fill it with a muslin pillow (see above) filled with the flower mix.

Padded Satin Lavender Coat Hangers

Little touches of luxury such as padded coat hangers can ensure your clothes last longer and hang well. Take a wooden coat hanger and cover with a length of wadding material measuring 90 cm x 5 cm (36 in x 2 in) and wind it around the coat hanger, stitching at each end. Cover the wire hook with ribbon and stitch to the wadding.

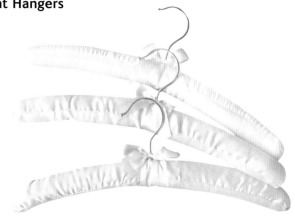

Cut out a piece of satin about 12 cm (4¾ in) wide and slightly longer than the hanger and fold lengthwise, sewing it across both of the short sides. Place the hanger inside the fabric casing with open edges on the top and temporarily secure with pins. Sew the seams with a running stitch, leaving the ends loose and then pull both ends to create a gathering effect. Tie a sachet of lavender to the hook and decorate with a ribbon. Your clothes will be perfumed and well cared for.

Lavender Ink

In these days of email and texting, it is relatively rare to get a handwritten letter in the post. An added pleasure for the recipient would be the sweet smell of lavender ink.

Crush 15 g/½ oz/heaping ½ cup dried lavender flowers and put in a saucepan with 6 tablespoons water and simmer for 30 minutes until the liquid is brown and reduced to around 2 tablespoons. Strain the liquid through some muslin and mix in with the ink.

Lavender Stationery

Perhaps one of the simplest – but surprisingly effective – ways to scent stationery is to store it in a drawer with lavender sachets. You can also soak a ball of cotton wool in lavender oil and store it in a box with stationery (taking care not to stain the paper) and leave for a few days.

For sweet-smelling wedding invitations, seal a few buds of dried lavender inside the envelope.

Lavender Glycerine Soap

Make some fantastically fresh and aromatic soap for yourself or even as a gift for someone else.

Put 500 ml/18 fl oz/2 cups lavender flower water (steep fresh lavender flowers in boiling water for 10 minutes, then strain) in a glass bowl over a pan of boiling water and add 500 ml/18 fl oz/2 cups glycerine and half a bar of grated, unperfumed white soap. Then add a handful of dried lavender and rose buds. Pour the mixture into a rectangular china dish and cool for at least 2 days before cutting the soap into bars.

Make Your Own Lavender Eye Pillows

Try making these lavender eye pillows to banish puffiness and ease headaches. Simply cut a 25 x 25 cm (10 x 10 in) piece of silk and fold the right sides together and stitch together with a small opening at the end, turn the silk right side out and fill with 170 g/6 oz/1 cup flaxseeds (linseeds) and 15 g/½ oz/heaping ½ cup lavender buds.

Lavender Candles

Make your own lavender candle by breaking up and melting 900 g/2 lb paraffin wax in a bowl over a pan of boiling water.

CAUTION: Keep the heat low as paraffin is highly flammable.

Remove from the heat and add 2 coloured wax crayons and 50 g/ 2 oz/2 cups dried lavender or some drops of lavender essential oil. Coat the candle moulds with petroleum jelly and drop a length of wick into each mould so it touches the bottom. Pour in the candle wax when it changes to a gel consistency and leave to set overnight. Remove from the mould the next day.

Lavender-Scented Holders

Add some fragrance to tea lights by placing them in a glass holder sprinkled with crushed lavender buds, taking care to raise the tea light above the lavender so there is no fire risk. As the tea light burns you should get a wonderful aroma of lavender.

CAUTION: Never leave burning candles unattended.

Special Occasions

Lavender can add a sweet fragrance to special occasions. Dried lavender can be used in wreaths, table decorations, Christmas tree decorations, dried flower bouquets and even strewn underfoot at outdoor summer parties. You can capture the fragrance of summer in dried lavender mixes and use in indoor topiary to be enjoyed in the depths of winter. Burning dried lavender in a wood fire on a cold winter's evening not only gets the flames roaring but releases a relaxing aroma too.

Lavender for Weddings

Bouquets

Add lavender to a bridal bouquet – it makes a stunning accompaniment to roses. In the *Victorian Language of Flowers* lavender is the flower of devotion and roses the flower of love. Lavender is also believed to be lucky – so a good luck charm for a happy marriage.

Wedding Keepsakes

After the big day the lavender and roses can be pressed as a keepsake or dried lavender added to the bridal gown storage box to help keep moths at bay.

Perfume the Ceremony

Bridesmaids can also scatter dried lavender and rose petals up the aisle, releasing the scent of lavender as they are crushed underfoot.

Decorate the Church

Tie bunches of dried lavender with big white bows of satin or ribbons to decorate each row of chairs in the church or wedding venue.

Lavender for Christmas

Make a Lavender Wreath

You'll need sprigs of dried dark purple lavender (*see* page 146 for harvesting tips). Glue Spanish moss to a wire wreath frame and cut the lavender to 5 cm (2 in) stem lengths, and then divide into bunches measuring 2.5cm (1 in) in diameter. The stems should be trimmed to 5 cm (2 in).

Then work your way around the circle, attaching them to the frame with floristry wire until it is completely covered. Secure the stems of the last group of lavender under the flowers of the first group of lavender that you secured to the wreath.

Use your wire to secure a loop for hanging on the back of the wreath. Add a large purple satin bow to finish off.

Lavender Christmas Tree Balls

The sweet smell of lavender conjures up memories of summer, but is also a good accompaniment to wintery smells, including spicy cinnamon, orange and cloves. Use it to make Christmas tree decorations and dried flower displays.

This is a simple trick – just remove the tops of clear plastic tree balls and push in dried lavender. You can also fill muslin bags with lavender, cinnamon sticks and cloves, tie them with seasonal red and green ribbons, and hang them on your fragrant pine tree.

Lavender Parcels

Decorate your gifts with sprigs of dried lavender instead of bows for a personal touch.

Christmas Table Decorations

Keep it simple. Mix dried lavender stems with deep red roses and holly sprigs. Add some pine branches for more aroma. Spray some pine cones gold or silver and place amongst the blooms.

You can also sprinkle dried lavender buds on the tablecloth to release a relaxing aroma to calm the inevitable Christmas tensions.

Lavender Log Fires

Fill your home with the welcoming scent of lavender wood smoke for a special occasion by saving dried stems of lavender and using them as kindling to start a wood fire. Add rosemary and twigs to create an even headier aroma.

Kitchen & Cupboard

The Basics

Have you explored the possibilities of lavender in cookery? Lavender has many beneficial properties, which have been overlooked in culinary terms. A delicious cup of lavender tea will relax both the mind and spirit as well as restore energy and wellbeing. Lavender can adapt to all sorts of recipes, from being used in salads to decorating cakes.

Hints and Tips

Lavender's Versatility in the Kitchen

Lavender can be used to add colour to a salad, marinade meat, lightly infuse panacottas and ice cream and add a sweet taste to cookies and cakes. It is also used as salad dressing, cake decoration, bread, biscuits, custard, sorbets, jellies, chocolate and even in vodka and champagne. There are few herbs that are so versatile and it's really worth experimenting with. The only word of caution is that it is a strong flavour so it's best to use tiny quantities so the flavour is not too overwhelming.

Choosing Lavender for Cooking

Many specialist shops now sell culinary grade lavender – using this is a good short cut if you're pressed for time. If you are going to pick your own from the garden – *lavandula angustifolia* (English lavender) is said to taste best. Also make sure that your lavender has not been sprayed with any pesticides.

Harvesting Lavender for Cookery

Experts say it's important to harvest lavender just as the buds are beginning to open – early on in the flowering season – if it is picked too late the taste will be bitter. Use your common sense and pick the healthiest looking stems and avoid those that are wilting or woody. The best time to pick them is in the morning after the dew has dried but before the midday sun has dried up any of the oils. Put the stems in water in a cool place until you need to use them.

Preparing Lavender

When using lavender, ensure that the leaves or flowers are pesticide free. Wash the sprigs thoroughly. When baking, chop both dried and fresh very finely to release the aromatic flavour, as does bruising the sprigs. Experimenting with lavender in the kitchen can be great fun – it's probably best to start with small amounts and then adjust to taste.

On the Grill

In place of wooden skewers, use dried lavender stems. Soak the stems for 10 minutes, thread the food onto them, then toss on the grill. You'll get to enjoy a nuance of lavender flavour to your food. Alternatively, put a few lavender stems on the barbecue coals to give your meat an aromatic lift.

Cake Decoration

Crystallized lavender flowers make beautiful cake decorations. To make the mixture for coating the flowers, whisk 1 egg white with 1 teaspoon of water, then using a small paintbrush, paint over each individual lavender flower with the egg. To finish, sprinkle some caster (superfine) sugar over the flowers and leave to dry overnight on baking paper. Once set, store in an airtight container.

Salads

It may not be the first ingredient you think of, but lavender flowers can make a great addition to your salads, and add a beautiful splash of colour to them too.

Basic Recipes

Lavender Sugar

It is incredibly easy to make lavender sugar. Simply fill a jar with a screw-top lid with caster sugar. Bury 1–2 fresh or dried lavender sprigs in the sugar and screw down the lid. Leave for 2 weeks before using.

You can top up the jar with more sugar until the lavender loses its potency then start again.

Lavender Tea

Lavender tea is reputed to be very beneficial as it helps to relax the body, alleviate stress and restore energy. Simply place a few sprigs of dried lavender in a teapot and pour on boiling water.

It can also be made by adding a few sprigs of dried lavender to a pot of English breakfast tea. Leave to infuse for at least 4 minutes then strain and serve, preferably black.

Recipes

With its sweet flavour lavender makes an excellent addition to recipes, and can really make a dish come alive, as well as making a beautiful garnish. Why not try some refreshing, yet easy-to-make lavender lemonade, some delicious lavender muffins or perhaps try your hand at making some strawberry and lavender jelly? Once you've discovered the magic of lavender, you'll want to impress with these recipes time and time again.

Lavender Crème Brulee

Serves 4

300 m l/^{1}/$_2$ pint/1^1/$_4$ cups double/heavy cream
300 ml/^{1}/$_2$ pint/1^1/$_4$ cups single cream
2–3 fresh lavender sprigs
4 medium/large egg yolks
4 tbsp caster/superfine sugar
Fresh lavender flowers, to decorate (optional)

1   Preheat the oven to 170°C/325°F/Gas Mark 3.

2   Pour both creams into either the top of a double boiler or into a mixing bowl stood over a
    pan of gently simmering water. Add the fresh lavender sprigs. Heat gently until hot but not
    boiling. Remove and allow to cool for 10 minutes, then remove and discard the lavender.

3   Beat the egg yolks with 1 tablespoon of the sugar until thick and creamy, then slowly pour
    in the cooled cream. Strain into the cleaned double boiler or mixing bowl.

4   Return to the heat and cook, stirring throughout until the mixture is thick and coats the back
    of a wooden spoon. Pour into 4 individual 150–ml/^{1}/$_4$–pint ovenproof dishes. Place on a
    baking tray and cook in the preheated oven for 5 minutes, or until a skin has formed on top,

5   Remove from the oven and cool then chill in the refrigerator for at least 3 hours,
    preferably overnight.

6   Next day sprinkle the remaining sugar over the top of each custard. Place under a preheated
    grill. Cook, turning the custards frequently until the sugar melts then caramelises. Remove and
    chill for a further 2–3 hours before serving, decorated with fresh lavender flowers if liked.

Lavender Lemonade

Makes about 900 ml/1¹/₂ pints

4 large ripe lemons, preferably organic
1 orange, preferably organic
50 g/2 oz/¹/₄ cup sugar, or to taste
2–4 dried lavender sprigs
600 ml/1 pint/2¹/₂ cups boiling water
Few fresh lavender sprigs
Lemon slices, to serve

1   Wash the fruits thoroughly and dry. If not organic, scrub the fruits well to remove any residue pesticides then dry. Using a vegetable peeler, pare off the zest and place in a bowl. Squeeze the juice from all the fruits and pour over the zest then sprinkle with the sugar.

2   Add the lavender sprigs and pour over the boiling water. Stir well then cover and leave overnight. Stir occasionally.

3   Next day, strain the juice off the zest and discard the zest. Pour into glasses. Add ice if liked, and place a fresh sprig of lavender in each glass and a slice of lemon on the side.

Lavender and Rose Butter

Makes 225 g/8 oz/1 cup (2 sticks)

2–3 fresh lavender sprigs
225 g/8 oz/1 cup (2 sticks) unsalted butter, softened
1–2 tsp rose water
Fresh rose petals, to decorate (optional)

1 Thoroughly wash and dry the lavender and chop finely.

2 Place the butter in a mixing bowl and add the chopped lavender and rose water. Beat with a wooden spoon until completely blended.

3 Spoon into a small serving dish and chill for at least 30 minutes before decorating, if liked, then serve. Cover with cling film/plastic wrap if the dish has no lid. Store in the refrigerator. This butter is delicious spread on scones, crumpets, toast or warm crusty bread.

Lavender and Lemon Squares

Makes 9

1 tsp oil
175 g/6 oz/^{3}/$_4$ cup (1^1/$_2$ sticks) unsalted butter, softened
175 g/6 oz/1^1/$_2$ cups caster/superfine sugar, plus extra for sprinkling
2 tsp finely grated lemon zest, preferably organic
1–2 tsp finely chopped dried lavender leaves or flowers
3 medium/large eggs, beaten
150 g/5 oz/1 heaping cup self-raising flour
25 g/1oz/scant ^{1}/$_4$ cup ground almonds
1–2 tbsp lemon juice, preferably organic

1   Lightly oil and line a 25.5 x 20.5 cm/10 x 8 in shallow oblong cake tin/pan with baking
    parchment or greaseproof paper. Preheat the oven to 190°C/375°F/Gas Mark 5.

2   Place the butter and sugar with the lemon zest and the chopped lavender in a mixing bowl
    and beat until soft and creamy. Gradually add the eggs with one tablespoon of the flour,
    beating well between each addition.

3   When all the eggs have been added, stir in the remaining flour together with the ground
    almonds. Mix to form a soft dropping consistency with the lemon juice. Spoon into the
    prepared tin and level the top. Sprinkle with a little caster/superfine sugar.

4   Bake in the preheated oven for 25–30 minutes, or until well risen and a skewer inserted into
    the centre comes out clean. Remove from the oven and leave to cool in the tin. Once cool,
    turn the cake out onto a board, discard the lining paper and cut into squares.

5   Store in an airtight tin.

Lavender Shortbread

Makes 12

175 g/6 oz/¾ cup (1½ sticks) unsalted butter, plus extra for greasing
225 g/8 oz/2 cups sifted plain/all-purpose flour, plus extra for dusting
125 g/4 oz/⅔ cup caster/superfine sugar, plus extra for sprinkling
1–2 tsp finely chopped dried lavender leaves or heads

1   Lightly grease 2–3 baking trays with a little butter or use non-stick tray liners. Preheat the oven to 170°C/325°F/ Gas Mark 3.

2   Place the flour into a mixing bowl together with the butter and rub together with the fingertips until the mixture resembles fine breadcrumbs. Stir in the sugar and chopped lavender. Using your finger tips mix together to form a firm but pliable dough.

3   Knead lightly until the dough is smooth then roll out on a lightly floured surface to about 5 mm/¼ in thick. Using a 5 cm/2 in or 7.5 cm/3 in fluted cutter, cut out biscuits/cookies and place well apart on the buttered or lined baking trays. Prick lightly with a fork and sprinkle with a little caster/superfine sugar.

4   Bake in the preheated oven for 15–20 minutes, or until a light golden colour. Remove from the oven and allow to cool for a few minutes before transferring to a wire cooling rack until cold. Store in an airtight tin.

Lavender Macaroons

Makes 6–8

1 tsp oil
1 large/extra-large egg white, plus extra for brushing
125 g/4 oz/²/₃ cup caster/superfine sugar
50 g/2 oz/scant ¹/₂ cup ground almonds
1–2 tsp dried and finely chopped lavender leaves or flowers, plus 4–5 dried flowers
150 ml/¹/₄ pint/²/₃ cup whipped double/heavy cream
Lavender sugar, for decorating, optional (see page 171)

1   Preheat the oven to 180°C/350°F/Gas Mark 4. Lightly oil and line 2 baking trays or use non-stick tray liners.

2   Whisk the egg white in a perfectly grease-free mixing bowl until stiff and the meringue does not move when the bowl is turned upside down.

3   Add the sugar a spoonful at a time and whisk well after each addition. When all the sugar has been added, stir in the ground almonds and finely chopped lavender.

4   Place spoonfuls onto the prepared trays, smoothing the edges and leaving plenty of space between each macaroon (to allow for expansion). Brush lightly with a little egg white and place a small piece dried lavender flower on top.

5   Place in the preheated oven and bake for 20–25 minutes, or until the macaroons are firm to the touch and light golden brown. Remove from the oven and allow to cool before transferring to a wire cooling rack. Store in an airtight tin.

6   Sandwich together with whipped cream just before serving and, if using, sprinkle with lavender sugar to decorate.

Lavender Cupcakes

Makes 12

For the sponge:
125 g/4 oz/^{1}/$_2$ cup (1 stick) unsalted butter, softened
125 g/4 oz/^{2}/$_3$ cup caster/superfine sugar
2 medium/large eggs, beaten
125 g/4 oz/1 cup self-raising flour
25 g/1 oz/^{1}/$_4$ cup ground almonds
2–3 tsp finely chopped dried lavender leaves
2–3 tsp cooled boiled water

For the icing:
225 g/8 oz/2^1/$_4$ cups icing/confectioners' sugar
3–4 tbsp warm boiled water
Few fresh lavender sprigs

1   Preheat the oven to 180 C/350 F/Gas Mark 4. Line a bun tin/pan with paper cases and put to one side.

2   Beat the butter and sugar until light and fluffy, then gradually add the eggs together with a spoonful flour after each addition. When all the eggs have been added stir in the remaining flour with the ground almonds and stir lightly together.

3   Add the finely chopped lavender with sufficient hot water to give a smooth dropping consistency. Spoon into the paper cases, filling about two-thirds full. Bake in the preheated oven for 20–25 minutes, or until the cakes are well risen, golden and firm to the touch. Remove and leave to cool.

4   Blend the icing/confectioners' sugar with sufficient hot water to give a smooth spreadable icing. Spread over the top covering completely. Serve when the icing has set, and decorate with a few fresh lavender flowers. Store in an airtight tin.

Lavender Muffins

Makes 9

350 g/12 oz/scant 3 cups self-raising flour
175 g/6 oz/1½ cups caster/superfine sugar
1 tbsp finely chopped dried lavender leaves or flowers
2 medium/large eggs, beaten
150 ml/¼ pint/²/₃ cup milk
50 g/2 oz/4 tbsp unsalted butter, melted and cooled
Few fresh lavender flowers, to decorate

1   Preheat the oven to 190°C/375°F/ Gas Mark 5. Line a muffin tin/pan with muffin paper cases and put to one side.

2   Sift the flour into a mixing bowl and stir in the sugar and dried lavender.

3   Beat the eggs with the milk and melted butter then gradually stir into the dry ingredients. Stir well then spoon into the muffin paper cases, filling about three-quarters full. Place a piece of lavender on top.

4   Bake in the preheated oven for 20–25 minutes, or until well risen and golden brown. Remove and cool in the tin or on a wire rack before serving. Store in an airtight container.

Lavender Ice Cream

Makes about 750ml/1¹/₄ pints

300 ml/¹/₂ pint/1¹/₄ cups whole milk
50 g/2 oz/¹/₄ cup caster/superfine sugar
3 fresh lavender sprigs
2 medium/large eggs, beaten
300 ml/¹/₂ pint/1¹/₄ cups double/heavy cream

1   If using an ice cream maker, place the bowl in the freezer the night before, otherwise set the freezer to rapid freeze according to the manufacturer's instructions.

2   Pour the milk into a saucepan and stir in 1 tablespoon sugar and add the lavender. Bring to just below boiling point then remove from the heat, cover with the lid and leave the milk to infuse for at least 3 hours.

3   Remove the lavender and discard. Beat the eggs with the remaining sugar until creamy then slowly pour the flavoured milk onto the eggs, stirring throughout.

4   Strain into a clean pan and cook, stirring with a wooden spoon, until a custard consistency that coats the back of the spoon is formed. Remove the custard from the heat and allow to cool.

6   Whip the cream until softly peaking, then stir the cooled custard and cream together. Either pour into the ice cream maker, following the manufacturer's instructions or pour into a container suitable for freezing. Freeze for 1 hour, remove and stir well, and return to the freezer. Continue to stir the ice cream at least three more times, in order to break up any ice crystals.

8   The ice cream can be served immediately if made in an ice cream maker or allowed to soften in the refrigerator for 30 minutes if frozen in the freezer. Serve scoops in small glass dishes.

Lavender & Strawberry Jelly

Fills about 4 x 450 g/ 1 lb jars

1–4 kg/4 lb ripe strawberries
Small bunch fresh lavender, thoroughly washed
150 ml/¹/₄ pint/²/₃ cup lemon juice
1 litre/1³/₄ pint/4 cups water
Allow 450g/1 lb preserving sugar for every 600 ml/1 pint/2¹/₂ cups extracted juice

1   Assemble the jelly bag over a bowl and scald with boiling water both the bag and bowl. Discard the water. Wash the jars to be used in hot soapy water and rinse thoroughly to remove the soap. Dry then place in a hot oven for 10–15 minutes, or until dry.

2   Thoroughly wash the strawberries, discarding any that are badly damaged or bad. Hull and cut any large fruit in half. Place in a non–reactive saucepan with a lid and add the lavender sprigs and lemon juice and water. Bring to the boil, then reduce the heat to a simmer and cover with the lid. Cook for 20–30 minutes or until the strawberries are soft.

3   Leave to cool for 10 minutes, then pour into the jelly bag so that the juice will drip into the bowl. Cover the top with a clean towel and leave in a cool, draught–free place.

4   When the juice has dripped through, measure the juice and pour into the preserving pan. Add the measured sugar.

5   Place over a gentle heat and cook, stirring frequently until the sugar has dissolved. Bring to a rapid boil and boil for 10–15 minutes, or until setting point is reached. Draw off the heat and cool before pouring into warm sterilised jars and covering with a waxed disc. When cold secure with a lid and label.

Index